The Land of My Fathers

T0037657

THE BASQUE SERIES

BOOKS BY ROBERT LAXALT

The Violent Land: Tales the Old Timers Tell

Sweet Promised Land

A Man in the Wheatfield

Nevada

In a Hundred Graves: A Basque Portrait

Nevada: A Bicentennial History

A Cup of Tea in Pamplona

The Basque Hotel

A Time We Knew: Images of Yesterday
in the Basque Homeland

Child of the Holy Ghost

A Lean Year and Other Stories

The Governor's Mansion

Dust Devils

A Private War: An American Code Officer
in the Belgian Congo

The Land of My Fathers: A Son's Return to
the Basque Country

THE LAND OF MY FATHERS

A Son's Return to the Basque Country

ROBERT LAXALT

Illustrated with photographs
by Joyce Laxalt

University of Nevada Press ▲▲ Reno & Las Vegas

The Basque Series   Series Editor: William A. Douglass

University of Nevada Press, Reno, Nevada 89557 USA
Copyright © 2000 by Robert Laxalt
Photographs copyright © 2000 by Joyce Laxalt
published with the permission of the Basque Studies Library,
Getchell Library, University of Nevada, Reno
All rights reserved
Manufactured in the United States of America
Design by Carrie Nelson House

Library of Congress Cataloging-in-Publication Data
Laxalt, Robert, 1923–
The land of my fathers : a son's return to the Basque country /
Robert Laxalt ; illustrated with photographs by Joyce Laxalt.
p. cm. — (The Basque series)
ISBN 0-87417-338-8 (cloth : alk. paper)
1. Laxalt, Robert, 1923– — Journeys—France—Pays Basque.
2. National characteristics, Basque. 3. Pays Basque (France)—Social life
and customs—20th century. 4. Basque Americans—France—Pays Basque
Biography. 5. Mountain life—France—Pays Basque. I. Title. II. Series.
DC611.B319L39 1999   99-34731
944'.79—dc21   CIP

The paper used in this book meets the requirements of American National
Standard for Information Sciences—Permanence of Paper for Printed
Library Materials, ANSI Z39.48-1984. Binding materials were selected for
strength and durability.

Some chapters of this book have been previously published, in somewhat
different form: "A Flight of Doves" and "Good and Evil Joust on a Wine
Glass," in "Land of the Ancient Basques," *National Geographic Magazine*
(August 1968); "Invaders" and "Tree of Gernika," in *Chillida at Gernika*
(Commissioned by Tasende Galleries, La Jolla, California, 1988).

ISBN 978-1-64779-154-4 (paper)

This book has been reproduced as a digital reprint.

frontispiece: Sheep on a country lane in Soule. *Joyce Laxalt*

For my father, Dominique

The Basque spirit is indefinable.

—LAURENT APEZTEGUY

There is one word which covers all the
qualities that go to make up Basque character.
That word is insularity.

—RODNEY GALLOP

It is even doubtful if the Basques
understand themselves.

—ANONYMOUS

The tiny homeland of the Basques—barely a hundred miles in diameter—straddles the crest of the western Pyrenees Mountains between France and Spain.

It is a land of deep oak forests, green mountain valleys, and the rugged seacoasts of the Bay of Biscay.

In these mountains and on these shores dwell an ancient people called Basques. Where they come from, nobody knows. They probably wandered into the Pyrenees millennia ago. Many Basques claim they are the pure descendants of Cro-Magnon man, who evolved in an isolated setting here, fiercely resisting all invaders. This assertion has received some support from scholars working with archaeological, linguistic, and most recently DNA evidence, but no one has yet come to an incontrovertible conclusion.

One thing is certain. The Basques are a distinct people who by blood and language are unrelated to the Indo-Europeans who dominated the rest of Europe.

The mystery of their origins has never been unlocked.

In his *A Book of the Basques,* British historian and folklorist Rodney Gallop lamented the lack of books having to do with the nature and character of the Basques. The two reasons he gave for this gap in history were the impenetrable reserve of the people and the reluctance of those few Basque writers to talk about the makeup of their ancient race.

Literature and history were not lacking in their views of the Basque character. Writers of antiquity depicted them as "fierce and turbulent barbarians." Scholar Le Pays described them as "always laughing, joking and dancing. Joy begins there with life and ends only with death." There were also detractors. One historian described them as "spiteful and vindictive and full of prejudices." A Norman pilgrim, Aimeric Picaud, went even further. He said the Basques were "black, perfidious, faithless, corrupt, violent, savage, given over to drunkenness and evil living." Picaud's intemperance may have stemmed from the fact that Basque brigands had relieved him of his valuables when he crossed the Pyrenees.

Rodney Gallop knew whereof he spoke. Unlike so many others who wrote about the Basques, he had lived long in the Basque provinces. His conclusions portrayed the Basques as "a people of loyalty and rectitude, dignity and reserve, independence and a strong sense of race, a serious outlook tempered by a marked sense of humor, a cult of tradition, a deep rooted simplicity and a courageous view of life."

I spent the greater part of two years, 1960–61 and 1965–66, in the Basque Country, along with my wife, Joyce, and our three children. Nearly all of that time was spent in mountain and seacoast villages, where I gathered many impressions about the Basques and their homeland.

As a son of Basque-born parents, I was not to be put off by the famous Basque reserve. I was readily accepted by family and their friends. There is a saying that one Basque cannot lie successfully to another Basque. I found that to be true. My aim of penetrating the true Basque character, its strengths and its weaknesses, its good deeds and its shortcomings, was fulfilled.

The traits and secrets of the Basque people and their robust minds are contained in these impressions. They are my offerings in understanding the nature and character of my people. Rodney Gallop would be pleased.

THE LAND OF MY

FATHERS

The sound of the distant horn came fluting up the brackened slopes. In the half-light of the rude tree hut, the Basque hunter held up his hand for silence. The sound of the horn came again, and this time the note of warning in it was unmistakable.

"So now it begins," he said. "You had better go down."

Three of us were cramped in the Tower of Death, a tiny tree hut perched in the topmost branches of a giant oak. The floor we stood on was piled with whittled wooden projectiles shaped like small paddles. Far beneath us in this high mountain pass of the Pyrenees was an old stone cabin with a sagging roof whose slates were green with lichen. And beyond the cabin, strung on poles that towered fifty feet into the air, hung a sweep of nets so fine as to be almost invisible.

This was the *palombière* of Lecumberry, in the French region of Basse-Navarre. The *palombière*, place of doves, is one of a dozen locations in the high passes of the Pyrenees on the border between France and Spain. Here, for many hundreds of years, the Basques have netted the wild dove in its autumn migration from the Scandinavian countries to the warmer climes of Spain and Africa.

As my Basque cousin Bertrand and I descended the dizzying ladder from the tree hut to the ground, the peaceful scene below was transformed into one of furious activity. Villagers in black berets were scrambling out of the cabin, some to dive into camouflaged mounds that held the levers to trip the great nets, others to conceal themselves behind a wooden barricade.

Through the eye-slit in the barricade, I saw the flight of doves—dark specks in a broken arc—coming swiftly into the funnel of the pass. When they were so near that I could hear the drumming of their wings, the white wooden projectiles lanced out of the Tower of Death like falcons whirling down in attack. They are thrown by hand to frighten the doves.

The flight reared up like a single thing, and then, to protect itself, dived close to the ground and came the rest of the way to the nets in a blur of swiftness. When the doves struck the nets, there was a soundless explosion of feathers. Birds hung in awkward disarray in the webbed strands as though they had been pasted against a canvas of sky. Then the levers were jerked and the nets came tumbling down. The air was rent with a spine-chilling sound that once had been a Basque war cry, and the villagers descended upon their catch.

They picked their way carefully over the delicate strands of the fallen nets to extricate the doves. Some would be cooked and eaten immediately, but most of the hundreds caught would be penned to provide fare through the winter months ahead. And for every one captured, thousands would pass the Pyrenees in safety.

Afterward, my cousin Bertrand and I went down the mountain, walking under a crimson-and-gold canopy of beech and chestnut trees in the full color of autumn.

"Did you find it cruel?" he asked.

I shook my head. "No, I found it old and tragic, and in a way I can't explain, beautiful."

"Good," said Bertrand. "Then you have not lost your Basque heritage by being born in America."

Only then did he explain to me the aspects of religion and poetry that accompanied the hunt. He told me of the Mass of Thanksgiving offered in the village churches at the end of the hunting season. Then, in that unself-conscious way of people who are raised with song, he sang the tribute the Basques had always offered to the beauty and pain of the dove.

Urtzo churria, urtzo churria,
Errani zaddack othoiegina
Nundat buruz haundonen . . .

White dove, white dove,
Tell me if you please,
Where were you traveling,
Your route so straight,
Your heart at ease?

From my country
I departed with the thought
of seeing Spain.
I flew as far as the Pyrenees,
there lost my pleasure
And found pain.

The wild-dove hunt of the mountain Basques symbolized to me the essence of this ancient race whose origins and language are obscured in mystery.

Though the age-old isolation of the Basques is breaking down, I had seen a primitive tradition that had managed to survive the centuries. In that misted mountain pass, I sensed a warrior ancestry that still lived.

We had broken now out of the mist, and the scene

that unfolded below us was like that of a hundred valleys throughout the seven provinces called Eskual Herria, the Land of the Basques. In the slanting rays of the late sun, the white waters of the Lauhibar coursed along the valley floor. On the green mountains, distant houses of whitewashed stone were bordered on one side by vineyards and on the other by the tiny figures of grazing sheep.

In a little village at the base of our mountain, white buildings with red-tiled roofs clustered around the steeple of a church. A man wearing a black beret with a wooden staff on his shoulder was walking ahead of two plodding oxen and a cart with great wooden wheels. The scents of greenery and moist earth rose up around me. Then unexpectedly the church bell in the village tolled the hour, and the melancholy sound nearly brought tears to my eyes.

This was the Cize region in Basse-Navarre, where I and my wife and children were to spend most of our two long sojourns in the Basque Country. In the neighboring valley was the village where my mother was born, and beyond the high range in the distance the rugged mountains where my father was born. This was the country of my people's beginnings.

The Basques are not much for words.
Theirs is a language of the eyes.
—Old Saying

The wooden pens beneath the lichen-covered ramparts were nearly filled with bawling calves, squealing pigs, and bleating lambs. The last of the Basque *paysans* with animals to sell were trooping in through the mists from farms scattered about the green countryside.

Today was Market Day in the central village of Saint-Jean-Pied-de-Port, where an open-air market on the main street has been held for so long that nobody knows when it started. Always, it is held on a Monday. The Sunday before is given over to the religious and the familial, with Mass in the morning, a family lunch at noon, and Vespers in the evening.

But Market Day on Monday is a different matter. It is a day of reunion between villagers and country folk, the animated business of buying and selling, handball and jai alai, courting and dancing. It is also a day when the Basque character sheds its silent reserve and reveals itself in a hundred ways.

The *paysans* are dressed in warm coats against the autumn morning chill. They are gathered in little groups marked by climbing wisps of cigarette smoke, and their talk is unusually animated. All are involved in reaching a common accord for what they will demand for their calves, pigs, and lambs. An accord must be reached before the livestock buyers from Bayonne and Biarritz descend upon them like buzzards preying upon the peasants' perennial poverty.

As if by arrangement, the buyers arrive at the same hour. They, too, reach an accord on time of arrival, so that no one will have an advantage when it comes to bartering with the *paysans*.

When the buyers arrive in their trucks, they seem all to be dressed in the same way—long, gray linen coats, glasses to make themselves look more businesslike, and a pocket full of pencils. The pencils are for show, because every transaction is performed orally and by the traditional hand slaps that are their way of shaking hands on an agreed-upon price.

The buyers are mostly Basques from the business centers of Bayonne and Biarritz on the sea, where avaricious bartering is a science. They all seem to have long noses, narrowed eyes, and downturned mouths. There are no smiles. For them as well as the *paysans*, bartering is a serious business.

When a buyer first approaches a *paysan* and his penned animal, he never stops to barter but goes on with a sideways glance of contempt for the animal, whether it be a calf, a pig, or a lamb. That is always the opening gambit, and the *paysan* accepts it with a small smile.

When the dozen or so buyers have made their tour of the pens, they huddle near one of the trucks and reach an accord of their own. They are practiced at prices, and the meeting does not last long. When it is done, they disperse according to their specialty in animals and descend again upon the *paysans*.

I watched one transaction in particular from beginning to end. Women almost never intrude upon the men's market, which by tradition is their husbands' domain. Raising the animals and planting corn and wheat have always been the responsibility of the *etxeko jaun*, or master of the house. The conduct of the household and the raising of children fall to the mistress of the house, or *etxeko ander*. A Basque husband may never criticize his wife's cooking or the cleanliness of the house.

But on this Market Day, a woman had usurped her husband's right and stood by him at their allotted pen. She wore a look of no-nonsense determination. The pen contained a calf, which to my little-trained eyes was a beautiful animal—dun colored, a rich coat, large but with no belly to speak of, which meant on the surface that the calf had never tasted grass. He had been raised to serve the palates of gourmets who had a taste for milk-fed veal.

The early return of a buyer was proof that the *paysan* had something of value. The buyer's first pass by the pen had been one of expected contempt, but his early return was more friendly. Still, his eyes and speech belied that. He was one of the breed that the Basques call *sharp trader.*

The buyer opened the ritual with a greeting and an inquiry into the *paysan*'s health and well being. To his annoyance, the *paysan*'s wife said, "If you intend to ask about our children's health, that is for me to answer. But first you must address the question to me."

"I apologize, Madame," the buyer said. "I haven't met you before. But that is not unusual for a men's market."

The jibe did not change the wife's demeanor. There were things that could have been said, but she chose to let the jibe go by.

The buyer had seen at first glance that the *paysan*'s calf would make for superior veal. But that was not enough to risk paying good money unless he was absolutely sure. He went inside the pen and examined the calf carefully with the usual narrowed eyes. That done, he felt the calf with knowing hands, finally lifting the tail to see for himself whether the calf had eaten grass. Satisfied, he said, "I won't play games with you. Your calf is a good one, and I am prepared to pay. How much are you asking for him?"

With a sideways glance at his wife, the *paysan* named a price. She nodded shortly in approval.

The buyer reacted as if he had had a seizure. His hands went up into the air with the accompaniment of a mock scream. "Preposterous!"

Taking a cue from his wife, the *paysan* affected a stone face and said nothing.

"All right," the buyer said. "That price is out of the question. What is your bartering price?"

"There is no bartering price except the one I gave you," the *paysan* said.

"And your absolutely unchangeable final price?"

The *paysan* shook his head. The buyer got out of the pen and went his way, muttering that he had a family to support, too.

"He'll be back," the *paysan*'s wife said.

"I'm not so sure," the *paysan* replied. He was watching the buyer close a deal with his neighbor for another calf with the traditional three clashes of their palms.

But the buyer did come back, once he had seen that the calf he had bought had been led into his truck.

"Listen," the buyer said. "I want to be reasonable. You saw the calf I just bought from your neighbor at a price higher than you reached in your agreement on selling prices. I am prepared to top even that price by 5 percent. What do you say?"

The *paysan* raised his hand to make the first hand clap toward the sale. A sharp exclamation from his wife stopped him, and he let his arm drop to his side.

"You are the first woman I have ever encountered in what is a men's market," the buyer said, but the wife was already looping a rope around the calf's neck.

"Then there should be more women involved." She accosted her husband openly. "Come," she said. "We are going home."

The buyer surrendered in what seemed to be genuine agony. He raised his hand and repeated the *paysan*'s first and only asking price. Their hands met in the three claps, and the transaction was done.

When the buyer was gone with the calf, the *paysan* said, "You had no right to shame my pride."

"When there is money needed to support a household, pride is not involved," the wife said. Out of the bills the buyer had handed her, she took one and gave it to her husband. "Go and have a Pernod or two with your friends," she said. "It will heal your wounded pride."

On Market Day, the women's market is in the afternoon. In contrast to the argument and tempers of the morning, the women's market is a peaceful one.

The farm women who come in from the countryside wear print dresses, except for widows who are bound to wear black for a year. If their farms are not too far distant, the women walk to Saint-Jean-Pied-de-Port. Others who live a distance away ride donkeys and mules, and some who have more than they can carry come in little one-horse buggies. Only a few come in flimsy Peugeots, the French equivalent to America's early Model T Ford.

The women who walk carry baskets filled with fresh farm eggs buried in oats to keep them from breaking, or fresh vegetables picked that morning. Others carry a squawking, upended chicken with its feet tied, and sometimes two squawking chickens.

The farm women come to market to visit as much as to sell. The few contents of their baskets, which are deposited on wooden counters in the improvised stalls against the ramparts, are easily disposed of. But each transaction takes time because the women must visit.

They have grown up and gone to school together. A husband's health, a child's sickness, and marriages in the offing all must be talked about.

When the eggs and vegetables and chickens have been sold, the farm women go to other stalls to buy such things as needlework and embroidery. New recipes for lamb stews, *confit de porc,* and marinated wild pigeons—a specialty of the region—are exchanged. And of course, the farm women and the village women must visit.

One part of the village's main street is subtly isolated. It contains small vans loaded with merchandise that will be displayed on the vendors' own counters. The vendors are a breed of gypsies called *bohèmes,* and except for market, they are excluded from the affairs of the villagers. Their stalls are loaded with things that are difficult to obtain in the village—work pants and sturdy shoes and rubber boots for the men, *tabliers* or school smocks for the children, print dresses for farm women to work in, and a variety of spices for the kitchen.

There is no exchange of amenities or bartering when the farm women buy from the *bohèmes.* They simply examine what is for sale—be it a straw hat for summer or a well-made apron for the kitchen—ask what the price is, and pay without comment.

All during the women's market, the young have an existence of their own. Scrubbed and combed farm boys and girls in bodices and red sandals and head scarves walk in groups seemingly oblivious to each other. But always, they manage to encounter each other on the streets of the village. Their meetings are shy, and there is laughter in them. Romances are often born in these not-so-chance meetings, and they will be furthered when the *Toro del Fuego* fireworks are over and the evening is filled with dancing of the *jota* or *fandango* in the village square.

The dancing goes on to the accompaniment of flute and accordion, and daughters are watched closely by their mothers sitting at sidewalk cafés. Meanwhile, husbands and fathers have gone to the indoor handball court or the jai alai *frontón* to wager or applaud or deride the skills of visiting players of reputation.

When the dancing and handball and jai alai games are done, it is time for the *paysans* and the farm women to go home. This time, husbands and wives go together, talking with each other about what transpired with them on Market Day.

The young also wend their weary way home, but their minds are occupied with more important things for them, such as dancing eyes and bright smiles and an unexplained quickening of their hearts. The ground is being sown for another generation of Market Days.

COMMON GOAL

Take three Basques who have agreed on a common
goal. Two will work toward that goal. One will work
against it out of principle. They hate unanimity.
　　　　　　　　　—Old Saying

In November, the Basque fishing fleets put out to sea
from villages along the Bay of Biscay. Their destination is the western coast of Africa, to which the tuna
schools have migrated from Basque waters.

Their day of departure is one of excitement and
celebration, beginning with the booming of cannon.
The quay is crowded with families of the fishermen —
old widowed grandmothers in black dresses and
scarves, wives and children, and girls waving goodbye
to sweethearts.

On the brightly colored fishing boats, ruddy
Basque sailors in blue turtleneck sweaters and yellow
oilskin pants divide their time between their work and
shouting hoarse farewells to their loved ones. They are
valiant men, and there is no gainsaying that they are
good providers for their families from the money they
will share at the end of their six-months' stay in for-
eign climes.

Little is heard about the wives who stay behind.
Theirs is the task of keeping a household, feeding a
family, acting the absent father's role as disciplinarian
to children, coping with emergencies and injuries,

bargaining with butcher, baker, and cobbler, and finally, worrying that their husbands will survive storms at sea without being washed overboard with no chance of rescue.

Though all attention is focused upon the fishermen this day, it is the wives who are the unsung heroes of a fishing village.

LAW

If you don't believe in a law,
don't break it. Simply sidestep it.
—Old Saying

Even the Romans in their conquest of empire never did try to subdue the fierce Basques, but formed an alliance with them instead. In 200 B.C., they exercised only token sovereignty over the Basque homeland and its diverse tribes that had banded together against a common invader.

None of the succeeding invaders after the Romans were victorious in conquering the Basques or erasing their identity. Vandals, Visigoths, Franks all encountered ferocious resistance from Basque warriors who waged guerrilla warfare on foot or mounted on shaggy ponies and then melted into their deep oak forests and mountains.

Tradition has it that hardened Germanic armies were appalled at the aspect of Basque warriors who threw themselves on their spears rather than surrender, and the still more unnerving practice of Basque sons creeping through the enemy lines at night to slay their own captured fathers so as to save them from the shame of being held prisoner.

The leaf is rusted now. Its original green hue is barely discernible. But that is natural, after resting for thirty years in its original hiding place, my wife's Missal.

The fringes of the oak leaf are like old lace that has yellowed with age. The texture is shot through with an intricate network of tiny veins that once carried the nourishment of life to the extremities of the leaf.

Despite the long confinement, the symbol stamped upon the leaf has not changed. It is clearly visible, the lofty trunk with its flowering crown and the two elongated wolves crossing the trunk. The physical substance of the symbol is firm, and its spiritual meaning has not weakened with the passage of time.

The leaf was given to us in the shadow of the Tree of Gernika, that ancient shrine of an ancient people, the Basques. Concealed in an envelope, it was slipped to me surreptitiously by a man in black, from beret to broadcloth suit to sturdy black shoes. He was a quiet man with a blade face and a fragile, finely arched nose—features that were unmistakably Basque.

Before he approached us, I had seen that he was scrutinizing me out of that unrevealing face. He recognized me as Basque, which is not difficult. But trust was another thing. Though Basque I was, he could see by my clothes that I was not of the country.

Something of my emotion in seeing the shrine of my ancestors, which had survived a thousand years of monarchs and tyrants and wars, must have transmitted itself to him, and in the end he made his decision.

His eyes stared into mine piercingly, judging whether I could be trusted. Not a word passed between us, but I knew I was not to open the envelope there but conceal it quickly.

I had thought to put the envelope in my pocket, but instinctively I passed it to my wife, Joyce, and she inserted it in the pages of her Missal. The Basque nodded his head in approval and went back to his self-appointed guardianship of the shrine. I am not given to credibility in matters of coincidence, but nevertheless the leaf by the merest of chances was to lie on the page bearing the psalm: *Blessed is the nation whose God is the Lord.*

The Basque in black took a terrible risk, chancing imprisonment or worse by doing what he did. There were Guardia Civil patrolling about. The year was 1961, and the time was in the darkest days of oppression by the Spanish dictator, Francisco Franco. It was a tyranny that had vowed to stamp out every vestige of the

Basques' culture: their code of human rights, their flag, their coat of arms, music and dance so old that they still contained pagan overtones, and even their language.

The prisons of Spain, and the graveyards, were, in 1961, filled with those Basques who refused to abandon either their language or their sacred *fueros*, the rights of man that Spanish monarchs for six centuries had promised to uphold. Even King Ferdinand V and Isabella after him had gone to the Province of Viscaya in 1476 and paid homage—under the spreading branches of the Tree of Gernika—to Basque rights.

The emotions that the Tree evokes from pilgrims are strong. For the Basques, the Tree of Gernika represents *order in life, strength, endurance, immoveability, dignity, loyalty to heritage, defiance to tyranny—all the sources of inner renewal most vital to survival as an individual and as a race.*

TRAGEDY

Tragedy is not in the Basque manner.
Death means nothing to us. That's life.
—Anonymous

The Basques deplore weakness. Yet they thoroughly enjoy seeing or hearing about those Basques who break the rules of conduct.

For example, José María's brother has a much younger girl as his companion this day. Eliza, my cousin, says, "Il faut pas regarder." "Don't look," and hides her face with her hands as she laughs at the misconduct of José María's brother.

The village feast in Iholdy is well and widely known, and visitors come a long distance to view it. That is because it is different.

Unlike the solemn processions and Masses on feast days elsewhere, the *Fête Dieu* at Iholdy is marked by clamor and outright noise. Apart from that, the *Fête Dieu* has ancient overtones that strike an unexplained chord in Basque folk memories.

The first symbol of ancience that a visitor encounters is greensward. Before the procession begins, grass is strewn in a wide path from village square to church and back again. It makes for a brilliantly green carpet.

When the village church bell tolls, it is time for the procession to begin, and all three hundred inhabitants of the hamlet participate.

The procession is led by bandsmen with drums and cymbals, fifes and cornets in a blast of sound that commands everyone's attention.

The bandsmen are followed by young men dressed in the uniforms of Napoléon's *Grande Armée*, blue with white sashes crossed on their chests, and tall bearskin helmets with small mirrors imbedded in the fur, which once blinded the foe when the Grand Army marched into the sun. Like their predecessors, the soldiers carry long muskets, gleaming swords, and lances.

Then come the Basque dancers, virile youths dressed in white with red and blue sashes, red berets trimmed in gold thread, and leggings with tiny tinkling bells. The dancers leap and twirl in the air and perform wondrous footwork on the greensward path.

Village girls with red skirts and black bodices and colored head scarves come next, singing joyous Basque songs in pure soprano voices. They are followed by children who scatter flower petals in front of the priest's entourage. The priest is dressed in his very best gold-hued robes and carries the Sacramental Host in a golden monstrance. He walks under a canopy borne by four acolytes in long red robes.

Finally come the villagers, women in black dresses and men in black suits, white shirts, and black berets. Their passing marks the end of the procession.

Inside the church, the middle aisle is taken by the participants in the procession—bandsmen, dancers, singers, flower girls. The priest and his entourage go up into the sanctuary for the conduct of the Mass, and the villagers separate according to tradition—the women in the nave and the men in the balconies above.

The women sing the priest's part, and the men sing the responses. Together, they make a counterpoint of soprano and the deep tones of baritone and bass.

While the Ordinary of the Mass is the same as elsewhere, there is a dramatic difference in Iholdy when the moment comes for the Consecration of the Sacramental Host.

When the priest turns to the congregation and raises the golden monstrance, three things happen. The soldiers aim and fire their muskets in a crashing volley that fills the church with white smoke from blank cartridges. The warriors raise their swords and spears overhead while they shout out their *irrintzina*, the piercing battle cry that Roman legions and Germanic tribesmen heard. The dancers line the railing of the sanctuary, and to the rhythm of flute and single-beat drum, dance a stylized dance altogether different from their dances in the procession. The dance is performed in ballet movements, stiff and constrained. The dance personifies what the Basques believe to be the most beautiful gift that they can offer to God.

The dance, they say, is older than Christianity. The origins of its symbolic meanings have never been traced.

But it is nevertheless easy to imagine that the dances

were once offered in worship of pagan gods. Its vestiges linger in the folk memory of the *Fête Dieu* in the tiny village of Iholdy.

The Basque song reaches its highest stage with the troubadour, or *bertsolari*. To be a *bertsolari*, one must have an agile mind as well as a good voice. The troubadours are not only singers but on-the-spot improvisers of verse who compete with each other in song.

In these encounters, the *bertsolariak* will argue any given subject—the good life of the sailor as compared to that of the mountaineer, the bachelor's life against that of the married man, the Basque who has stayed in his homeland and the Basque who has gone abroad.

I watched two of my favorites, Xalbador and Mattin, dispute in song at a village feast in Saint-Étienne-de-Baigorry in France. Xalbador is a lean-faced Basque who affects in contest the pose of someone slightly tipsy. His beret is pushed back on his head, so that his lank hair falls over his forehead. His forte is an attitude of droll cynicism toward life. Mattin is his opposite in every way. Short and round, he reminded me of Friar Tuck. But behind his jolly grin is a rapier mind.

It was an incredible performance. For nearly an hour, they exchanged quatrains with dizzying speed. At the end, it was impossible to know who had won out. But one thing was certain. The villagers who listened to them would have many delicate turns of phrase in the nuance-rich Basque language to relish for weeks afterward.

After Basque singing, one remembers Basque dancing.
One spring day, we joined a throng of people in the central square of the village of Tardets, my father's birth-
place, in the mountain province of Soule.

Early that morning, dancers had begun wending their
way down from where green meadows met the snow line,
dancing in each village along the descent. Their route
would end in Tardets.

They were performing the Dance of the Zamalzain,
the oldest Basque folk dance and one of the most ancient
in Europe. Once, it must have been a pagan fertility
dance to celebrate the coming of spring. It is a dance of
good against evil, beauty against ugliness, and man's eter-
nal battle to conquer his circumstance.

We were standing with my cousin Petya. "As you will
see," he said, "the Zamalzain is a very difficult dance. In
order to do it properly, one must begin when he is ten
years old."

As we spoke, the crowd parted and the dancers came
into the square to the accompaniment of music from the
txirula, a shrill Basque flute played with one hand while

the other beats out a heartbeat rhythm on a drum called an *atabal.*

There were two troupes of dancers. One was resplendent with dazzling costumes, and the other was dressed in shapeless rags and hideous face masks.

Petya explained: "One troupe represents good and beauty, and the other evil and ugliness. But in this dance, good does not always conquer evil. The beautiful dancers must make the good win out. Keep your eye on the goblet of wine in front of the dancers."

In turn, one of the beautiful dancers and one of the grotesque dancers approached the wineglass. The beautiful dancer stood erect, with his upper body held rigid and only his legs in motion.

In time to the shrill music, his sandaled feet skimmed above and around the wineglass so closely that it trembled. When he backed away, the grotesque dancer went through the same routine, but in contrast to the other, his motions were purposely disjointed. Still, he did not upset the goblet either.

The laughing good humor and the applause of the onlookers faded into silent apprehension as the dance reached its climax. This was when the Zamalzain, the leader of the beautiful dancers—whose waist was encircled by a wooden framework representing a tiny horse caparisoned with velvet and lace—danced toward the wineglass. His lightning feet performed their movements around the glass, and then suddenly he leaped onto it and as quickly soared into the air and away. The glass rocked violently, but it did not spill.

Then the king of evil approached the glass. His slovenly dancing mocked the perfection of the leader of the beautiful dancers. His sandals landed firmly on the edges of the glass, but when he leaped away, the glass fell over and the red wine spilled.

There was a huge sigh of relief from the villagers, and then wild shouts of approval. Beauty had triumphed over ugliness, good had conquered evil.

As we walked down the lane toward my cousin's farm, I exclaimed, "I can't recall when I've been so nervous as waiting for the outcome of this dance, of all things."

"Well, it's more than a dance," said Petya. "It's an omen. What happened today portends good for the year." He grinned self-consciously. "I know that in these times one is not supposed to put much stock in such things. But still, one cannot escape feeling better inside when the omens are good."

Bells passing my cousin's farmhouse at night tell us they are contraband sheep, or else they wouldn't be moving at night. Night is the time when the *contrabandiers* practice their profession, moving sheep and cattle and mules back and forth across the frontier between France and Spain.

FRILLS AND FANCY

Basques don't like frills and fancy, or at least the country-
men don't. It is their nature to prefer things practical. In
this, they differ so from their neighbors in France—the
French.

Sitting beneath me in the high mountain chapel are the women. They are indistinguishable from each other in their black dresses and black scarves that hood their heads.

In the embracing somberness of the ancient chapel, only the altar stands out. Against the gloom, it is a blinding backdrop of brilliant colors—golds and purples and reds.

On the sanctuary wall above the altar is a gray-haired God holding the world in His hands. He is not a God of easy compassion. Taking away His long hair and flowing robes, He would have fit well in the gallery of men's faces that looked down on Him from the balcony.

Basques are intensely curious. They regard you with inquiring, inquisitive eyes that carry a concealed brooding, as if nothing is new to them.

A thousand years and more ago, my Basque ancestors erected the stone chapel that was our destination. The high peaks and crests of the Pyrenees Mountains abound in chapels and pagan monuments that serve in our day as ends for pilgrimages from the valley floors.

In my father's high mountain province of Soule, we had climbed a tortuous trail to a monument of mystery, the Chapel of the Madeleine. There is a Christian altar there now whose origin can be explained, but there is also an almost indecipherable stone marker inscribed in Latin letters. The shrine is dedicated to Heraus, the Basque Goddess of the Red Dust. Legend has it that Basque warriors worshipped at her shrine before battle. Nothing else is known about her.

When Christianity finally managed to replace paganism, the stone chapels were renamed after saints. The mountain crests became the road to Santiago de Compostela in Spain. Along this road, pilgrims could take shelter in comparative safety from Basque brigands who had moved down to the valleys below. It took a long time for the Basques to exchange their symbolic paganism for Christian worship, and vestiges of it still remain.

Another pilgrimage, to the Chapel of Saint-Sauveur

high on the mountain above the valley where we were living, was for what is called the Shepherds' Mass. Once each summer, shepherds come to the Mass from their little stone huts lying in sheltered pockets near where their sheep are grazing. Villagers, mostly women and children, make up the procession from the villages below, giving the pilgrimage a holiday and picnic air. Even black-shawled grandmothers lined the route, hardly impeding the pace of the procession. Children, for whom the long climb was a lark, gamboled in front. They carried backpacks and shoulder slings filled with bread and cheese, sausage and wine, for the picnic that would follow the Mass. Only a few of the village men, mostly shopkeepers, made the seven-mile trek.

When we reached the first turn in the trail, we could look down on the white villages on the green valley floor. And directly across from us was one of Europe's last oak forests of consequence, Iraty.

Oaks mixed with chestnut and birch trees created a forest so thick that it resembled a green mound that wound down like a waterfall into the grassy ravines. The divisions between forest and grassland were as sharply etched as if they had been cut by a razor. Above the timberline, grass flowed unbroken over the mountain barrier between France and Spain, tipping onto a great rock face opposite from us like a monk's tonsure. Low-hanging clouds hung in wreaths across that face on the mountain.

The Chapel of Saint-Sauveur came in sight, nestling in a depression with its back almost flush against the mountain. It was a structure of little round stones from creek beds and sharp-edged stones from rocky ledges, all fitted together. Over the centuries, lichen had formed against the walls, giving a greenish cast to the grayness of the stones.

Shepherds began appearing from their own chosen routes down the grassy slopes above the timberline, where their flocks grazed on the summer feed. There were a few moments before the Shepherds' Mass was to begin. The shepherds gathered in little groups, smoking hand-rolled cigarettes of strong black tobacco from which the smoke rose in spirals. They visited with each other, catching up with what had happened of importance in their isolated little domains on the great mountain. Once, the priest—a rotund and jolly Friar Tuck—moved through the groups with joking humor.

There was no uniformity at all in the shepherds' dress. One man had on a thick wool shirt buttoned to the neck and covered with a brown coat. Another shepherd had on an old striped suit with high lapels. It was so worn that one had to assume it had belonged to his father and probably his father's father. Black coats and brown coats and mismatched pants made up the dress of the others. They shared only two things among them. One was sturdy black shoes with thick soles. The other was a shared discomfort at having to dress up for the Mass.

A tinny bell sounded in the belfry, signaling the beginning of Mass. Last puffs of cigarettes were taken and the butts dropped to the moist earth. The two steps from the ground into the *balcon* where the men would sit were made of stone, with the tread of a hundred years and more worn into them. Each man nodded to the man in back of him and stripped off his beret. They nodded also at me, though I was a mystery they could not understand. My dress—tweed coat and turtleneck sweater—said American, but my face was unmistakably Basque. Women and children entered a door on the ground level and filled the nave below.

Inside the *balcon*, there were long, narrow benches not five inches across, so that the men perched rather than sat. The benches had been shaped with an adze and worn smooth by a hundred years of sitting. There were no benches to kneel on, so the shepherds had to stand during the Consecration. The air was heavy with the smell of wet wool from a chance shower, but the shepherds themselves gave off no odor except that of mountains. The taller of the men had to stoop at certain times of the Mass if their heads encountered the slates on the roof.

Chinks of light came through the roof to lighten the gloom ever so slightly, and one slate could be moved to right from left if the shepherds wanted more air to breathe in the confined balcony. When it rained, the slate was closed.

From the balcony, we looked down on a little altar with what resembled a fried egg plastered against a blue background and an array of crude symbols that may have gone back to pagan times. The egg-shaped blob, of course, was a primitive sun.

Round faces, blade faces, florid faces, gray old faces, blue eyes, gray eyes, and brown eyes, white hair and black hair, red hair and blonde hair, and uniformly strong hands—and they were all recognizably Basque. For some unexplainable reason, it was as if they were all related and had been related since the prehistoric times when the Basques were a barbarian tribe inhabiting the same valleys as now. And that recognition included the likes of me, plainly an American but nevertheless Basque.

When the Mass had ended, and with it the beautiful counterpoint of soprano from the women below and the

44

baritone and bass of the men above, the chapel seemed to tremble from song.

Near the chapel, there was a *kayola*—a shepherd's hut—that had been converted into a rustic bistro. While the women and children picnicked on the grassy slope, the shepherds trooped through a low door and entered the bistro. They sat at hand-hewn tables and benches to take their rum and coffee. What light there was from a chink in the roof and two tiny window slits was almost obliterated by the smoke from the shepherds' cigarettes.

With rum and hot coffee in quantity, the shepherds' reserve seemed to melt away, to be replaced by songs. Not caring what the village women thought, my wife, Joyce, and I went inside and found a seat at one end of a shepherd's table.

They seemed determined to find something out about me. I accommodated them, saying that my father had been a shepherd boy in the Pyrenees and a sheepherder in the mountains of the American West. That established a common bond between us. Knowing that they were by nature and tradition storytellers, I told them about an incident in the American West that could have happened in the Pyrenees Mountains. After that, each had a story to tell and determinedly did so. Before it was over, I had gotten a dozen stories to write about in exchange for my one.

Daylight was waning by the time the shepherds' stories were done. They trooped out of the bistro and took their chosen trails back into the forest. Their gait was considerably slower than the springy steps with which they had come down to the Shepherds' Mass. Snatches of song drifted back down to us.

Joyce and I followed the last of the villagers down the mountain to the valley floor below.

A MEAN WOMAN

When a Basque woman is mean, she is venomous
and exudes it like a fishwife.

When first we came to the Basque Country, my relatives in the highlands would probably have apologized for the country lane, which was muddy from winter rains.

They didn't know what to make of me and my little family then. After all, we were from America, the legendary land of richness in all things. They were even a little uncomfortable, especially on the little farms in the province where my father was born.

We have been here long enough now for them not to change the way things are and to be easy in our presence.

We had been invited to a light supper in my cousin Petya's farmhouse. Two of my cousins who lived in the tiny village of Montory had decided to join us in our walk to Petya's farmhouse.

It is an old farmhouse with the year 1860 engraved in the keystone above the double front doors. The house is sadly in need of whitewash, but other tasks come first. The house has many narrow windows to let in the outside light. That and the reflection from the fireplace provide most of the light that comes into the house.

When first we entered and had exchanged greetings, we sat down in the kitchen at a long, scarred wooden table with benches on its sides. The table was set for a simple supper of soup, sausage and bread, and wine. The soup was prepared in a kettle hanging over the flames in an open fireplace that provided access from both sides.

Petya's wife is a buxom peasant woman with a ruddy, round face and pleasant hazel eyes. She is square and solid with strong forearms, and she is definitely feminine. As she leaned over the kettle in the fireplace, light from one of the narrow windows bathed her in near profile, so that she reminded me of a Vermeer painting of a Dutch farm woman.

Sitting in a corner of the kitchen on a Basque chair that is attached to a bench was the matriarch of the house. She was wearing widow's black and proclaiming for us her age, which was eighty-seven. She was jealous of another farm woman who was also my relative, and who was ninety years old.

The soup was ladled into our bowls from a tureen. It was a rich vegetable soup that had been bubbling since morning.

What intrigued me most was how the men at the table ate their soup. When the vegetables had been eaten and there was only broth remaining in their bowls, they poured wine to mix with the soup. Then they lifted the bowls and drank noisily.

This was something they would never have done at table in the beginning of our sojourn. The fact that they could drink their soup in the rude manner of the country made me realize a truth. So many doors had been opened to me because of the fact of family. It was a way of living that would never have been revealed had I been a stranger.

The Zhuberos of high-country Soule Province
don't think much of the low-country Manesh of
Basse-Navarre Province. They ignore them as soft.
The Manesh of Basse-Navarre respect the
Zhuberos of Soule but can't understand them.
—Old Saying

The priest at the Basque village of Arneguy is dead now, but his exploits live on. In his lifetime, he was known as a phenomenon, and justly so.

A big, bluff man with a gift for harassment, he would interrupt his own sermon by announcing that someone had stolen a chicken from his field the night before. Then he would point at a hapless victim among his parishioners and roar, "Martin, what were you doing in my field last night? I will bet that you were the one who stole my chicken."

Martin would protest his innocence, but the priest simply waved him aside. The nuns who were seated in the front row of the church would begin to giggle, and the priest would roar at them, "What are you laughing at? Maybe it was you who stole my chicken." It goes without saying that the priest's Sunday Masses were fearfully attended, but nevertheless attended. The Basques, who delight in irreverences, would not dare to miss the priest's outrageous behavior.

Apart from his antics in church, the priest was better known for another kind of behavior.

The village of Arneguy is a politically divided village.

One half of it lies in France, the other half in Spain. The illogical frontier runs right through the middle of town, dividing the duties of local government and family relationships. Even the church and cemetery are divided, the church in France and the cemetery in Spain.

When one considers that Arneguy was a single village for thousands of years, a line drawn down the middle as recently as 1530 makes no sense at all.

Sometimes, however, it serves a good purpose.

During World War II, it became an escape route to neutral Spain for American fliers who had been shot down over German-occupied France.

If the flier were lucky when his plane was shot down, the French underground would save him from capture by pointing him to a nearby farmhouse. The French peasants would hide him and give him food and shelter until the search died down. Then the peasants would disguise him in shabby clothes and point him toward the Basque-inhabited Pyrenees Mountains, which formed the frontier to neutral Spain.

At first, American fliers escaped by making a successful crossing through the deep forests along the mountain frontier.

It did not take long for the Germans to discover what was going on. They built a chain of little huts along the crest of the Pyrenees for their sentries to live in. After that, the frontier became a trap for would-be escapees.

It was the priest at Arneguy who solved the problem of how to pass the American fliers across safely. When a flier was shot down, the underground would guide him at great risk to a farmhouse on the outskirts of the village of Arneguy. The farmer would wait until the way was clear before taking him farther. First, however, the flier had to give the password that the priest at Arneguy had devised. The flier had to say, "The moon is red." The farmer would respond, "That's a strange color for the moon to be. The moon is really blue."

When the flier had passed the test, the farmer would take him to his destination at the house of the priest of Arneguy. The flier would be hidden until the next village funeral was in the offing. Then the flier would be dressed in the long robe and hood of an *enfant de choeur*, or acolyte. When the funeral Mass was done, the priest would give the flier a burning candle to hold during the procession to the cemetery, which of course was in Spain, across the frontier.

Once in Spain, the flier would wait until the funeral service was over and he was taken under the protection of a Basque in Spain. Later, the flier would turn himself in to the Spanish officials and eventually be sent to England on a fishing boat.

The Germans never discovered the ruse of the funeral procession. One young German officer new to Arneguy stopped a procession with a demand for identity cards. He was given a tongue-lashing to remember by the priest at Arneguy for interfering with a religious rite. The young German did not try again.

When the war ended, the priest of Arneguy shrugged aside the official recognition that military and civil authorities wished to confer upon him. But among the Basques, he will always be known as a folk hero.

The contraband horses that passed at night a few weeks ago were caught by the customs officers. They were not pretty horses, so they were probably meant for slaughter.

Now that the customs *douaniers* have them, it is required that there be an auction. At the auction, the only man who will bid will be the smuggler or a friend of his. This is tradition. The customs officers must accept the bid. But it cannot be too low. Among the Basques, even crime has its rules of fairness.

This also is tradition.

DUTY

A Basque's obligation to duty is so strong
that it is frightening.
—Old Saying

The wind was not blowing hard, but it was nevertheless blowing, its voice moaning through the bare branches. Suddenly, it would rise to a snarling that was wild and high and then fall to a rumbling growl from deep in something's breast. I have never seen a tiger in the jungle, but I imagine its sounds were like that.

The Basques call it *sorgina,* the witches' wind. It is a restless south wind that carries the troubling tempers of Spain and Africa with it.

On the seacoast, *sorgina* makes for a seething sea. The wind catches the crests of the waves and throws them back in a veil contrary to the movement of the sea. The sea cannot pursue its natural course when *sorgina* is blowing.

In superstitious times, people believed that when *sorgina* was blowing, girls would leave their houses when everyone was asleep. Wearing black shawls to blend with the night, they would meet and go down to the sea. Warm rain and warm temperatures would accompany them, and they would dance in nude and steaming bodies until their *sabbat* was done. Then they would steal home and crawl into their beds and fall into a dreamless sleep so deep that they could not remember what had happened during the night.

I have known *sorgina*, too. When it blew, I lay on my bed troubled with stirring passions. I got up and went outside to walk. A week before, the night was so cold that it was biting at my face. But that night, it was a warm wind blowing through me, and I could feel my blood in a turmoil that would not be stilled until healing sunrise flowed over me.

My cousin Eliza claims that the Basques have a masochistic nature. When it is time to work, the Basques approach it as though it were a flagellation. It is as if they are punishing themselves.

Eliza feels that the Basques want to sweat and toil in the old way. *By the sweat of your brow,* she claims the Bible says. If you are working for someone, you must give it your all, or it will not be money honestly earned.

But I know they are not punishing themselves. For them, work is a cleansing. The Basques derive pleasure from it. They emerge from work as if stepping out of a bath. There are smiles on their faces when a laborious task is done.

When it is time to play—be it at jai alai, handball, or the running of the bulls—they will play as hard as they worked. They will think of nothing else.

If it hadn't been for the crowing of a cock or the bleating of lambs, I suppose the German soldiers must have thought they were occupying an uninhabited land.

The German convoy was substantial, some four hundred soldiers—which would make it battalion strength. More than enough to keep order in a dozen tiny villages and *quartiers,* my cousins told me. But then, one never knows in wartime.

The convoy was led by an open-air Mercedes staff car carrying the commander, his orderly, and his second in command. Motorcycles with sidecars came next, carrying officers with stiff-billed caps, polished boots, and Luger automatic pistols. Finally, there was a line of troop carriers, the first and last ones armed with upraised and mounted machine guns to cover front and rear. The soldiers were combat-ready with steel helmets and rifles.

As had been the case with the hamlets they had driven through on their way from the seacoast to the Pyrenees Mountains, there was no sign of life in the main central village of Saint-Jean-Pied-de-Port. Streets were deserted, blinds pulled down on storefronts, and windows shuttered on the houses.

There was no one available to tell the commanding

officer where the offices of provincial government were. The Germans had to find out on their own. The instigators of this tactic wanted to show the occupying force that they were not welcome in Basque land.

My cousin Bertrand had opposed the tactic, saying it boded no good for relations between the occupying force and the people. "I argued that we had to live with the Germans, so why infuriate them?" Bertrand said. "There will be recriminations."

Bertrand, as it turned out, had reason to be worried. He knew that if the war went badly for the Germans, the young men of the village could be conscripted for labor camps in Germany.

When the convoy reached the courtyard with its statuary and three-storied buildings, it was waved to a halt by the officers. The troop carriers formed a circle around the courtyard, and the command car pulled up in front of what seemed to be the mayor's office. Still, no one came out to meet the commanding officer and his staff.

His irritation showing, the commanding officer led his aides up the steps to the mayor's office and opened the door. Luckily, Bertrand told me, it was open. If it had been locked, the Germans would have shot it open, Bertrand learned later.

There was one lone woman seated at a desk in the reception room. She displayed no emotion when the Germans strode up to her desk, but said simply, "Yes?" Afterward, she delighted in telling the townspeople how she had maintained the proper chilliness to the Germans, unlike the mayor.

The commanding officer did not deign to ask the obvious question, I could surmise. His aide, a secretarial-looking man, performed the task. "The mayor," he said. "We wish to speak to the mayor."

The receptionist inclined her head toward an open door behind her. "That is the mayor's office," she said, and went back to her papers. The Germans ignored the lack of an introduction and strode through the open door.

The mayor voiced a carefully guarded greeting of surprise, though he must have known who was calling. He was a short, rotund man with a graying moustache. His firmly set mouth relaxed into a polite smile, and he stood up. One look at the commanding officer's face told the mayor, politician that he was, that the village was overplaying its hand, exactly as my cousin had warned.

He waved the Germans to the chairs that stood in front of his impressive desk and asked what he as mayor could do to help them in their occupation.

The commanding officer nodded to his aide, who said as if by rote: "We will need four hundred beds for our soldiers, and two villas, one for the officers and one for the commanding officer."

The mayor was in a quandary. "That is a lot of beds for a village of this size. And where can I find two empty villas?"

"Evict the occupants," the commanding officer spoke up. "As for my men, they can be quartered here and in the hamlets surrounding this village."

"Of course, there must be provisions for feeding our men and us," the aide said sternly.

"Yes, of course," the mayor said in surrender.

"Fine," the aide said. "We will occupy our quarters this day."

The mayor suddenly found himself on the brink of becoming a very busy man, not only in delegating his own aides to distribute the Germans where he could and pleading with two irate families to vacate their villas. There was no other choice than to obey the Germans' occupying force.

Within a week, most of the Germans' demands had been met. All of the citizenry of Saint-Jean-Pied-de-Port and its environs had been tabulated by name. Adults were required to have identity cards. All guns had been turned over to the troopers designated for the task of collecting them, or so they thought. The best pistols and rifles had been carefully hidden. Fowling pieces could have been included, but the commanding officer relented and decided to exempt them from confiscation. Villagers and farmers alike depended considerably on wild game for food. German money had to be accepted by shopkeepers and bistros. Gasoline was reserved for doctors who owned cars. Curfew was set for 9 P.M.

Penalties for violating the rules would be handed down immediately, with the unspoken threat that serious breaches of the new law would mean jail or deportation to labor camps in Germany. To set an example, a German trooper who had gotten drunk in a bistro was the first man sent to jail.

When the new order had become routine, relations between the Germans and the Basques mellowed. The German troopers were under strict orders not to molest the village girls. There was not a single known liaison, except with the *bohèmes*, whom the villagers did not consider Basque and about whose welfare they cared nothing.

It was not an uncommon sight to see a sprinkling of Germans at handball and jai alai games. Indeed, both Germans and Basques used the same playing field for soccer. In the beginning, the German troopers were young and athletic. "We would have liked to play against them," my cousin Sauveur, who was an athlete, told me. "But that was against the rules, more the pity. We would have taught them a lesson."

The situation changed in 1943 when Hitler suddenly invaded Russia and opened up another front. Without advance notice, the occupying force in the Basque provinces of France was cut in half and the pick of the troopers were sent to the Russian front.

By this time, the German officers had learned something about the Basques. As they admitted to the villagers, they had found a people who could work as hard as they. And the Basques were Aryans without impure blood, as was the German elite.

Another cousin, Eliza, was generous in her praise of the Germans, a number of whom were housed on her and her neighbor's family farms. "They sang and laughed a lot, and they liked the children. They laughed when the children would imitate their goose-stepping and even when the children pinned tails on them before they drilled on the soccer field."

The amiable occupation began to fall apart when Hitler decided to attack Russia. Suddenly, Germany

needed every man it could find—both for the battle-
field and the home front.

A German officer who had become popular with the
villagers was the one who warned them of what was to
come. The first to be forcibly recruited would be the ma-
chinists and metal workers and carpenters. Then would
come the youth of the villages, young men between the
ages of twenty and twenty-five, who would be sent to
work camps in Germany.

This was to set off a minor exodus of workers and
young men who did not want to go to bomb-shattered
Germany. Those who chose to go were shipped off without ceremony. Those who chose not to go hid out in
barns and cellars or chose the dangerous route of escap-
ing to neutral Spain.

My cousin Bertrand was one of those who vanished
from view one day. He spent the better part of three
months without seeing the sun, hidden out in the musty
cellar of a centuries-old farmhouse. He went out only at
night, when the German troopers at the neighboring
farmstead could not see him. The troopers who had been
quartered in my cousins' farmhouse had been sent to
Germany.

The German officer who was friend to the villagers
became an informant for them. He alerted a trusted

man among the villagers and told him where and when the Germans would be patrolling the frontier. When the coast was clear, the young Basques were guided by the Resistance over old smugglers' trails across the Pyrenean rim into Spain.

The German officer elicited a promise from the villagers: "When my time comes, you must help *me*." And they did, hiding him, disguising him in Basque shepherd's garb, and guiding him across the frontier. He turned himself in to Spanish officials and was jailed for six months as a token gesture to the Germans.

By then, it didn't matter. Germany was to all effects beaten. The Allies had invaded Normandy, and their armies were halfway up Italy. The Russians were advancing. The remainder of the German troops in Basse-Navarre, now reduced to old men and boys, were shipped off to the Russian front to be slaughtered.

The time of occupation was ended. The Basque Country had survived another in a succession of invaders that had come and gone over nearly two thousand years. Modes of war had changed, but not the nature of the Basques. They could not have existed as a people without the quality of endurance.

From his earliest thinking years, he was known as an idealist. This quality did not endear him to the general run of the Basques, who pride themselves on their practicality.

He came from a very old and respected family in Basse-Navarre. In fact, his father was consul general of the commune for many years and was held in high esteem by the government of France.

Perhaps out of youthful rebellion against his father's close alliance with the French (I shall call him Etchebarne), he was an active separatist in the movement for Basque nationalism. He became almost fanatical in his zeal for Basque independence from the governments of France and Spain.

Then came World War II and the German victory over France, and the occupation of Basse-Navarre. Though the Basques did not openly sanction armed resistance against the occupation forces, the Germans knew exactly where the Basques stood—for opposition against anything German. When they learned about the Basque separatist movement, which was now dormant because of world war, the Germans sought to fan the flames of nationalism again. They did so by promising a Basque Country independent from France when they had won the war. Except for such as young Etchebarne, they found few recruits. As a one-time Basque separatist leader said, "We may be Basque, but we are French in that it is their country we live in, after all." He added that, "Separatism can wait until the Allies have won the war."

Young Etchebarne did not agree. Because the Germans had promised a free Basque state, his loyalties went to them. They received him with open arms. Since Etchebarne was a bibliophile, the Germans rewarded him by giving him private Basque libraries that they had confiscated.

In the beginning, Etchebarne had been discreet about his alliance with the Germans. Now, he took to consorting with them openly—dining and drinking with them and participating in their mock councils working out a separate Basque state.

Etchebarne's world turned over when the Germans began to lose the war. Sensing what was to come, he tried to join the occupying force when it went back to Germany. When they would have nothing of him, he finally realized that he had been used as a dupe.

His premonitions were accurate. When the Germans were gone, the provisional French military government arrested him and sentenced him to death. His father,

gravely ill, never knew that his son was to be executed by
a firing squad. For his sake more than anything else, the
father's friends argued for mercy for the errant young
man. His sentence was commuted, and he was sent to a
penal colony in Martinique for five years.

When Etchebarne came back to the Basque Country, he was labeled as a traitor and regarded with open
hostility by his countrymen. He became a recluse in
his family home and buried himself with his books.
Tentatively, he began to write, but never about his de-
fection and his penal servitude in Martinique. His
writings were published in a small review published
by a Benedictine monastery.

Gradually over time, the onus wore off, but never to
the point of acceptance by the Basques. He was merely
tolerated, and it showed.

It was at this time in his life that I struck up an acquaintance with him because of our mutual interest in
things Basque. I knew nothing about his background.
But in the Basque Country, nothing is secret for very
long. By then, he was a scholarly looking man with iron-
gray hair and a gray tinge to his skin as a reminder of his
years in a tropical penal colony. His face had many, many
wrinkles and deep grooves in it. In short, he looked his
torture.

Monks and fellow intellectuals were his only friends. The people of his own village tolerated him but would never forgive him. It showed in their eyes and was reflected in his own.

Though it came as a disturbing surprise that I could have done without, I learned then what I always suspected. The Basques are not vindictive, but neither are they a forgiving people.

When first we came to the Basque Country to live, the little house we rented was on a street leading to the rickety narrow-gauge railroad in Saint-Jean-Pied-de-Port. My cousins called the avenue the Street of the Americans.

This puzzled me because we had been led to believe we were the only Americans in the village. Also, I had perceived from a nodding acquaintance that our neighbors were obviously Basque. The houses they lived in were impressive villas, and this added to the paradox.

Finally, the mystery unfolded itself. The villas had been built in the 1920s and '30s by Basques who had lived in the United States, working as sheepherders for as long as ten or twenty years in the mountains and deserts of the American West. Unlike those Basques who had chosen to stay in America, they had come home to the Basque Country with their savings, gotten married, and started families.

My cousins explained to me that they were the offspring of *petits paysans*, which means *poor farmers*. They did not tell me that these Basques had gone to America to better their station in life. The uncharitable among the villagers still considered them *petits paysans*.

"They went to America because they couldn't succeed here," the uncharitable said, neglecting to mention there was no way the Basques could have succeeded in a land of no opportunity.

The Basques who had come back with money and built their villas consorted mainly with each other in the bistros and on village feast days, sharing mutual experiences in towns named Reno, Fresno, San Francisco, Los Angeles, among others.

That they were even being denied their birthright of being born Basque did not seem to bother them. When I talked to them, they simply shrugged their shoulders and smiled. They knew that the subtle ostracism was born out of envy.

REPUTATION

If a person's reputation is maligned,
it is never forgotten.

—Saying

A Lion Tamer

It would be easier to be a lion tamer than
to try governing the Basques.
—Old Saying

The village gossip was dying to find out what the American was doing. She would go so far as to know practically everything about him: what he liked to eat, what he liked to drink and how much, did he really take a bath twice a week, where did he go when he made his round of the village shops.

She even learned that the American was a writer, but she could not find out what he was writing about. The woman who cleaned his house couldn't tell her because she didn't understand English. Neither did the man who tended the garden.

The village priest told her, "The writer doesn't say, but I think he is writing about the people of our village."

Upon hearing this, the gossip clapped her hands over her ears and fled to her house. She had found a worse gossip than herself.

When one walks for the first time down a village street, the regard with which he is met by the Basques is like a physical force.

Yet one can live in a Basque village for a long time without seeing a single act of violence. From this, one would gather that the Basques are a friendly people. So they are, usually. But one should not make the mistake of thinking that they have only a peaceful nature. I have learned better.

It is a matter of common sense. The Basques are strong and passionate, but they keep their emotions concealed.

The tradition is: "There are few things in life that are worth a fight. *Laisser passer.* Let it go by. Ignore what is not worth an argument."

I have also learned why it is that Basques suddenly fall quiet in the middle of a conversation. The tradition is: "If a conversation is useless, don't listen. Just close up your face or get out."

If one listens to tradition, the Basques say, life can be made much more bearable.

Morning Mass and afternoon Vespers were done in the high mountain chapel where the people had come on pilgrimage. The villagers had started their long walk back down the mountain path to the valley, and the shepherds with their thin walking staffs had returned to their flocks on the other side of the mountain.

Only the priest and the girl remained to put the altar back in order.

The priest cocked his ear to hear if there were any voices outside the chapel. With his other ear, he heard the girl's drying of the cruets that had held the priest's wine and water for the Mass.

The priest called out, "Pantasha?"

"Yes, Father. I am here in the sacristy," the girl responded cheerily.

"Your mother and father have gone down the mountain," the priest said.

"Yes, I know," the girl said.

"I will take you down when you are done," the priest said.

"Yes, I told them you probably would," Pantasha said.

The priest went through the door to the sacristy and

closed it behind him. The cruets had been washed, and Pantasha was drying her hands.

The priest crossed the sacristy and opened the door to a little room with a cot in it. He went in and called out, "Pantasha."

"Not again, Father."

"You must obey your priest."

The girl surrendered and went into the little room with the cot in it. The priest closed the door.

When it was done, the priest said, "Now, you must remember to make confession to me next week."

"I will, Father."

Being an American without prejudices, I was curious about the role of the *bohèmes* in the Basque Country. Nobody seems to know where they came from and what blood they carried. They have been in the Basque Country for generations and always in a class by themselves. The Basques do not recognize them as Basque and tolerate their presence only to do menial chores, such as working in the fields, caring for the vineyards, and doing heavy housework.

Over time, they have learned to speak Basque and have forgotten whatever they spoke before. They live in hovels and at one time begged for handouts in the streets. The Basques did not tolerate this, so the *bohèmes* were forced to do menial chores to earn enough money to eat. The men and women fight often when they are drunk, and the gendarme must quiet them so as not to disturb proper people. *Bohèmes* marry *bohèmes*, never Basques. Yet they have adopted Basque names and can speak a rudimentary form of Basque. They are lazy on the whole and, according to the Basques, lack intelligence and any sort of ambition.

The village boys make rendezvous with *bohème* girls and lie with them in the forests. Sometimes, the *bohème* girls get pregnant. The village boys don't worry. There is no rule or law that they have to obey, because the girls are *bohèmes*, and therefore a race apart.

Of late, the *bohèmes* have taken to moving out into neighboring parts of France and Spain. They say they are Basque, but in doing so they give the Basques a bad name. Sometimes they even marry and bring their brides to the Basque Country, where there is a big surprise awaiting them. The *bohème* youth particularly like blonde women, probably because they are so dark themselves. Sometimes, the women stay with their husbands in the Basque Country, but more often they return to their homes, either with their husbands or without.

I have asked my relatives if the *bohèmes* will ever be absorbed into the Basque race. The answer is invariably an irate *No*.

I believe them, but over the course of time, I am not nearly so certain as they.

The family name of Arretalepho disappeared centuries ago, but the property retains the name of its founder. Despite their real names, all who live there have been called Arretalepho. They answer to it as a matter of course.

My cousin Petya does not know the proper name of the young man who married into the property when he wedded the eldest daughter, who was the heiress, contrary to what the Napoleonic Code calls the rule of primogeniture. Still, my cousin calls his neighbor Arretalepho when he meets him at market.

Because the name of the property is sacred, it is considered sufficient.

He drinks so much because he
fights a lot with his wife.
Whenever he wants to get drunk,
he arranges to have a fight with his wife.
—Cynicism

We had climbed above the timberline and a cloud bank that stretched out forever, so that we could not see the valley villages far below. It was like a new world. Great humps of bare mountain were covered with a green carpet of grass, broken only by outcroppings of white rock.

The rolling mountains that formed the frontier between France and Spain were dotted by flocks of sheep that shone brilliantly white in the clear air.

Each flock is tended by a shepherd and his shaggy dog. It is the shepherd's responsibility not to let his flock of fifty to one hundred sheep intermingle with the other flocks. This—in the brotherhood of Basque shepherds on the mountain—would be a grievous offense.

Also, the shepherd must send his dog at a run to keep the flock within the prescribed limits of communal grazing land. If violated, this would be an even graver offense against the code of the shepherds, which is severe indeed, as we were to learn.

The huts in which the shepherds live and make their cheeses lie in hollows of ground that protect them from the wind and storms. Also, they provide a view of that part of the mountain where the shepherd's flock grazes.

The shepherds' huts were built stone by stone perhaps as long ago as a thousand years. The bigger stones were laid first, and then a myriad smaller stones were pounded into the chinks. Whatever apertures remained were filled with clay. Basque barbarians who dressed in the skins of wild animals and carried spears probably dwelled in the huts. After the Romans brought sheep to Basque lands, shepherds used the huts for shelter and as vantage points to watch over their flocks.

I could almost feel the ancience of a hut and its primitive inhabitants when I stooped low to enter. When my eyes had grown accustomed to the gloom inside, I took notice of its construction.

A huge beam of oak supported the roof, which was covered with black slates so that no downpour could penetrate it. The roof inside was blackened with fire smoke that did not escape through a chimney. There was an open fire on metal plates near the entrance, both for cooking and for light. Two flat stones resting on the metal plates supported a fire iron shaped like a hairpin, on which frying pans and cast-iron Dutch ovens were laid. Hollowed-out niches to hold spices and coffee lined the hut. A ham and a bacon wrapped in white shrouds hung from the overhead beam. On one side, there was a bed frame of sturdy poles built against the wall. Bracken and a mattress served as layering for the shepherd's bed.

Outside, the hut was almost surrounded by an oval paddock into which the sheep were turned at night. It was made of wooden poles and wire and wooden cross pieces for a gate. On the other side of the hut, there was the shepherd's garden, where he or his helper had planted cabbage, carrots, and leeks. A running stream ran below the house, providing water for the shepherd, and lower down, a pool where trout could be caught by hand, with fingers thrust into gills before the fish was flipped out upon the bank.

The shepherd's day begins with the dawn and ends at nightfall. His first duty after coffee is to milk his sheep. He begins at one end of the paddock and traverses its length. He pours the milk into a mold with drawstrings and mixes rennet with it to make it harden. At end of day, he repeats the process and tightens the drawstrings on the mold. The skim milk that pours down a groove is part of the shepherd's diet.

The sheep are turned out of the paddock and herded by the shepherd and his dog to his allotted grazing land on the great mountain. He tends them carefully until they have lain down for their noonday rest, when he returns to the cabin to tend his garden and bring in firewood. He has his lunch of bread and cheese and wine— *ogi eta gazna eta arnoa*—when his flock is grazing again.

When the sheep have been penned at end of day, the shepherd has his dinner of pork or lamb, potatoes, and a vegetable. Then he sits back and enjoys a leisure time of smoking before drowsiness overcomes him.

He has little truck with the dozen other shepherds on the mountain. They are taciturn men who seem not to be bothered by loneliness. Yet they seem to know what each other is doing.

When a shepherd is seen beating his dog or handling his flock of sheep in a rough manner, he will be called upon to explain his actions. By some prearranged agreement, the other shepherds descend upon the recalcitrant together and hold court. If the shepherd refuses to apologize, he is given the choice of moving his flock to the next mountain or fighting with *makilak*, stout walking staffs. If he succeeds in vanquishing the first shepherd, he must fight the next in line. Inevitably, his strength gives out, and when he has recovered, he moves his sheep and himself from the brotherhood of shepherds.

I encountered one who was about to be called to a shepherd's court. I had gone for a hike to explore the big mountain so that I would know firsthand what the shepherd must contend with. I found out.

After losing my direction, I ventured into more unknown ground. My mountain calls were not answered, there was a mist moving in, and I nearly stepped over a precipice. I decided to follow a creek I had found to higher ground. In one clearing, I met a shepherd. He did not welcome me. When I told him what shepherd I had come up with and asked where his hut was, the dour shepherd refused to answer me. I went on my way, and eventually my call was heard and I found my shepherd's hut. It was then that I learned that the gruff shepherd who had refused to help me was about to be punished for his treatment of his animals. I could not muster any sympathy for him.

I had learned much in one day, including a lesson on how my father had lived when he was a shepherd boy in the Pyrenees. He had lived with taciturn and hard surroundings, but it had not affected him.

The Basque character is melancholy,
or satiric, or humorous.

—Anonymous

The Basque fishermen of the Viscayan villages that lie
along the Bay of Biscay are a powerful breed. Long years
of hauling in their catch from the sea—tuna, sardines,
and sharks—have given them piano legs and arms like
tree trunks.

When a fishing boat has docked, there is an ordered
frenzy of activity. While the men start to clean their ship,
the women take over.

They haul the catch to trucks that will take the fish to
the quay. There, in open-air market, they sell their wares.
There are buyers from restaurants, vendors, and a throng
of villagers shouting to be heard. The open-air market is
like the screeching of a hundred sea gulls, and the shrill-
ing voices of the fishwives arguing with buyers give them
their name of "fishwife." They stand by the trucks
guarding their husbands' catch, and no one in his right
mind would try to cheat them. They have arms that are
Herculean from many years of hauling fish, and they too
have piano legs.

They are different from the farm women in the
Pyrenees Mountains that hover in the distance. The wil-
lowy Basque farm women also work. They rake new-

mown hay into long lines, and this solitary endeavor
gives them quiet demeanors.

They pause statuesquely in the fields to watch my car
go by.

The Wind and the Rain

When the wind comes up at night, heralding a summer storm, all the world is filled with its force. Nature has assumed a single personality.

The wind is the voice of nature, sobbing and screaming in summer, sighing with a human voice in spring, moaning in autumn for the dying year, cold and vindictive as an outcast in winter.

The rains are the tears of nature, falling gently in the spring, suddenly and emotionally in summer, and sadly in autumn as it prepares the earth for the death of winter.

How I love the dawn. Above the mountains, the eastern sky is streaked and sooty, and I feel a moment of gray hopelessness.

And then the sun comes up and the gray, sooty streaks suddenly become beautiful—rose clouds and patterns in the frosty blue porcelain sky of a new day. Beech trees and their myriad tangle of branches are like cobwebs against the sky.

A newborn lamb in his manger mews, protesting the cold. The lamb follows its mother from the barn out to grass, and all his world is transformed. The farmer whistles as he opens the barn door, and the rest of the sheep trail out of the barn to the sound of tinkling bells.

The village below is still encased in fog, but the higher rooftops have caught the first light and are gleaming against the green hills and valleys that surround the village. Before the morning's light bathes them, they will guard their ghostly mysteries.

There is a *paysan* near the village of Saint-Jean-le-Vieu with a penchant for showing off his sheep, of which he has an impressive number.

Every Market Day, the *paysan* drives his band of sheep through Saint-Jean-Pied-de-Port, which is already congested on Market Day.

I have asked villagers why the *paysan* wants people to know how well off he is. When I thought about it, I understood why they looked at me curiously when I asked the question.

It is a matter of station, which is important to all Basques, Old World or New World. It is the reason why Basques who have made money in America come home with big cars. It is also the reason why the churches are not lacking for stained-glass windows with family names printed on them. The *Amerikanuak* want to show their neighbors that they have succeeded in this world.

MARRIAGE

A man who marries a first time is not quite bright.
A man who marries twice is an imbecile.
—Old Saying

The dreary time of winter is gone, and summer
is here and life has recaptured the Basques' earth
and their hearts.

In Europe, the institution of smuggling is as old as the concept of frontiers. So it is in the Basque provinces of Spain and France.

As far as the Basque Country is concerned, the traffic is not concerned with the so-called "little packets" of narcotics, with which the Basques will have nothing to do. It concerns liquor and livestock.

The profit motive is always there, but also involved is the challenge of a Basque *contrabandier* pitting his wits and wiles against those of the government, for which the Basques have an inherent indifference.

It is one thing to know and laugh about the business of contraband. It is another to learn how it works. I set out to do just that, despite the misgivings of a relative who had been a police *commissaire*. Though most of the known *contrabandiers* did not want to tell me the tricks of their trade, I found those who would.

"I will tell you something about how smuggling works for me in the Basque Country," one *contrabandier* said. "But you must promise to protect me. I am counting on your honor as a Basque not to use my name."

I gave him my promise (I was really not interested in his name, only his profession), and he went on.

"Let us start with the simplest form of smuggling," the *contrabandier* said. "That of liquor—Spanish brandy, sherry, and wine." He explained that liquors are cheaper in Spain, where there is no government control, as there is in France.

The *contrabandier's* partner in Spain hires as many as ten helpers to make the passage across the frontier into France. Each man carries twenty pounds in a goatskin container on a backpack. While the team is on Spanish soil, there will be no interference by frontier customs guards, since liquor is not in their jurisdiction. Also, it is going into France, so they are not interested.

The contraband passage is always at night. When the team reaches the frontier—a roughly defined no-man's land—it is fair game for French customs. The smugglers wear dark clothes—black berets, blue shirts, and blue cotton pants, the colors of night.

If he detects the passage, a French frontier guard fires his pistol into the air. The smugglers simply drop their goatskin bags and flee into the deep forests. The French guards confiscate the liquor, and the adventure ends there.

A more prosperous *contrabandier* told me about his traffic in livestock. "I moved mules and horses, and sometimes sheep. But sheep are too slow, so I specialize in Spanish mules."

The *modus operandi* was essentially the same as in liquor, but the obstacles and penalties were more complicated.

"Purposefully," he said, "I have conducted myself very properly for a few months, waiting for the French customs officers to let down their guard. You must understand that customs officers know who the *contrabandiers* like me are, so they keep an eye on me until they grow bored with the task."

The *contrabandier* said that when he decided it was time to make a run across the frontier from Spain to France, he would go to Spain and contact his partner there. "There is always a market for strong Spanish mules in France," he said.

He went on to explain that his partner in Spain would buy, say, twenty-five mules from those Spaniards who traffic in animals. "I give him $1,000 (in your money), and he buys the twenty-five mules at $40 a head."

His partner in Spain will hire three young men to take the mules over the Pyrenees mountain rim to the French frontier. He chooses his men carefully. "To be a good smuggler's helper," the *contrabandier* said, "a young man must have strong legs, sharp eyes, good ears and nose, and an elastic conscience."

If the movement is to be by day, then the *contrabandier* has the responsibility of choosing people along the route on the French side to alert his own team. They keep their eyes out for the French frontier guards whose job it is to detect the passage of contraband. His people can be shepherds, farmers, or young men pretending to be innocent hikers.

If anyone along the chain detects the French frontier guards, he will alert the next lookout by whistles and shouts if they are shepherds, or on foot, and so on down the line.

The strategy is to move the contraband mules over the frontier and the mountain to the valley land in France, where they will be put into a farmer's field. The field is private property, and the frontier guards must respect that right.

The wisest passage is by night, a stormy night when the rain is falling. The French frontier guards are not eager to leave the comfort of their huts to go out into a storm.

As with the liquor smugglers, he said, "My men make the climb to the frontier in dark clothes. If there is a storm, they will take along a dark *txamarra,* a short cloak that covers their upper body. They are difficult to detect, especially in the dark oak and beech forests I have chosen for the passage."

The *contrabandier* went on, "Each man on my team will take ten mules that are tied head to tail. They keep a distance of at least thirty yards between them and the next man."

If men and mules are not seen, it speaks for itself that all went well and good, he continued. If not, the game gets complicated and sometimes dangerous.

The guard will shoot his pistol into the air to summon help and to let the smugglers know they have been discovered. "My men drop the reins," he said, "untie the mules from each other, and shoo them into the forest where they will be difficult for the guards to round up. Then they themselves run into the forests they know so well."

Sometimes, though, the guard will be close enough to jump one of the smugglers. According to the rules, the smuggler has the right to defend himself with fists and feet in order to get away. If he is big and threatening, the guard has the right to draw his gun and make him prisoner. This is a rare circumstance, but there have apparently been some glorious battles between frontier guards and smugglers. If a smuggler kills a guard, then his life is forfeit.

"If one of my men is arrested and taken to jail," the *contrabandier* said, "it is my duty to pay his fine and get him freed. If my man has hurt a guard, he must appear before a tribunal and be sent to jail for six months. But usually a fine is sufficient."

My contraband informant has another task to perform if his mules have been caught and taken to the village. By law, there must be an auction of the mules. "But I will forestall that by going to the customs officer and saying, 'You've got my mules. I paid $40 a head for them. How much are you asking?'" They barter for a while and come to an agreement, and the *contrabandier* takes his mules home. He has lost most of his profit, but there are risks always in the illegal.

"If we cannot agree on a price," the *contrabandier* said, "then the auction proceeds. But it is an auction in name only, since my neighbors will not bid against me. I will be the only person to bid, and the customs officer must abide by the outcome."

. . .

Since my conversations with Basque contrabandiers, *the Common Market has almost done away with frontiers. This is as it should be, but I will bet that both* contrabandiers *and frontier customs guards must feel that something of the romantic past has been lost.*

Old Woman's Admonition

When you see me packing my valise, it will
be time for you to shine your shoes.

The reason the dictator did not persecute him was that
Castor came from one of Viscaya's first families and
was a wealthy man in the bargain.

Otherwise, Castor—who was a fervent Basque—
would have been a target for General Francisco
Franco. Not that Castor was involved in nationalist
causes, but he openly proclaimed the purity of the
Basque race. He reminded Basques of the day when a
couple could not marry in Viscaya unless they could
provide written proof of their pure Basque ancestry.

He was active in other ways, too, such as being a bene-
factor to the Basque Academy, an archive that had existed
for a century or more. Franco's hirelings could have inter-
ceded here, but they were reminded that the Academy
dealt with the Basque past, not the present. It was a delicate line to walk, but it avoided an open confrontation
with a man who had been decorated by the Pope in
Rome for dissolving his family's munitions industry for
humanitarian causes. Castor was then free to follow his
profession of architect.

Castor and I had met in the United States. When he
learned that I was planning a stay in the Basque Country

to write and study, he had extended an invitation to visit him and his family in Bilbao.

My wife and I had been greeted warmly and graciously. There was lunch at another Basque aristocrat's home (with serving girls wearing white gloves), folk dancing by the daughters of other old families, a cocktail party that included diplomats, a visit to Santamamina, the oldest known cave-art sites of charcoal drawings of bison and deer, and a somber tour of the restoration at Gernika, the peaceful Basque village that the German Luftwaffe had bombed at Franco's bidding during Spain's Civil War.

When these amenities had been accomplished, we returned to Castor's apartment building for dinner with his family. Castor and his wife occupied one floor of the building, his sons and their wives and children two other floors, and still another floor for Castro's daughter and her husband. It was like a family fortress.

Throughout all this, I was mystified at how close Castor's family was skirting the dictator's embargo of things Basque. But the true test was yet to come. At dinner's end, windows were closed and drapes were drawn when Castor rose to his feet and cried in Basque: *"Gora Euskadi!"* Long Live the Basque Country!

We raised our glasses and drank, and then Castor began to sing. His family followed him, and so did I, first in discreet tones that any Guardia Civil lurking outside could not hear. But as the forbidden Basque national anthem continued, passions could not be restrained. The voices rose in crescendo almost as a taunt to anyone listening:

> *Gernikako arbola da Bedeinkatua*
> *Euskaldunen artean guziz maitatua.*

> Tree of our Gernika,
> Symbol blessed by God,
> Held dear by all Basques,
> By them revered and loved.
> Ancient and holy symbol,
> Let fall thy fruit worldwide,
> While we in adoration gaze
> On thee, our blessed Tree.

And then, with unbridled passion, they sang:

> *Mille urte inguru da esaten dutela*
> *Jainkoak . . . arbola*
> *Zaude bada, zutikan orain da denbora*
> *Eroritzen ba'zera erras gaidu gera.*

> . . .

A thousand years or more ago—
So says race memory's voice—
The hand of God set deep thy roots,
Tree of Gernika.
Stand tall, great Tree, and do not fall.
Without thy boughs above,
Most surely will we come to grief—
Most surely we'll be lost.

As I listened, I remembered a story told me about a young Basque at the Fiesta of San Fermín in Pamplona.

The young man was singing a song in Basque at one of the downtown bistros. A Guardia Civil, armed as usual, forced his way into the bistro and told the young man that it was against the law to sing in the Basque language.

The young man, with flashing eyes, told the Guardia Civil, "You may stop my Basque song, but you will never stop my Basque heart."

When Castor's family, with tears in their eyes, had finished their singing of *Tree of Gernika*, I knew a truth. The dictator would never stop the beating of a Basque heart, but also, he would never still the song of the Basques.

The butcher and I were standing in the entrance to his shop, but my attention was drawn to two old ladies gossiping nearby.

One was still a pretty woman with white hair piled neatly on her head. The other woman's hair should have been white, but it was dyed black, and her face was mottled with the blue of heart trouble. They were talking with such loud voices and with so many gestures that they did not seem to be of the village.

The butcher explained to me that the two old women were indeed of the village, but they had spent many years of their lives as cooks in private homes in Paris. Whenever they chanced to meet, they always talked about the same thing—their experiences in Paris.

When their conversation had ended, the old woman with the dyed hair and blue skin crossed the village street and got into a little two-horsepower car that the French call a *deux chevaux*. As she started her engine, another little car driven by a merchant of the village came slowly around the corner. The old woman glanced back once to see if the coast were clear (which it was not) and put her gear into reverse. The two little cars met as gently as baby buggies in the middle of the street.

No harm was really done, but I could not help re-marking, "A woman like that should not be allowed to drive."

The butcher shrugged. "Why not? It's *his* fault. Everyone knows she is almost blind."

The diffusion of light in these mountains continues to surprise me. The rocky bluffs and sheer precipices above my mother's village, Baigorry, should be stark and brutal. But at dusk, they are violet and soft and inviting.

The man at Aldudes, sitting across from us in the café,
must be six feet across and three feet through. He has
massive bones covered with great slabs of muscle. And
over that, thick rope cords of tendons that jut out from
his neck. He has forearms like tree trunks, and you know
he can pick up a car if he wants to. He is blue-eyed, and
arrogant, and a man to avoid.

He is trying to assess what I am made of, trying to discover my weaknesses. He is completely confident with
women, as though he is the type of man all women want.
My wife turns and whispers to me in English, "That man
is lately emerged from the caves."

The country folks' year turns on the land. The land is their nurture and their livelihood. It must be treated with care and reverence.

Through the gray, rain-filled months of winter, the land had lain seemingly dormant. But underneath the stubble from last year's harvest, it had been gathering its strength for spring.

Spring is the planting season for the corn (maize), the crucial time on which the seasons turn. It is the time when the land that supports the little farms of the Basque countryside must be made ready for the harvest, so every number of the farm family is involved.

The days begin at dawn and end at dusk. In the morning, the night fog still lies over everything. Beaded veils of gray-white vapor lie across the steeple of the village church. As the sun burns it away, the fog rises from the ground and leaves stone fences glistening with dew.

No one is exempt from the planting time—fathers and mothers, sons and daughters, and even widowed grandmothers who shed their black dresses and don well-worn skirts. The men wear sturdy boots, and their wives wear print work dresses for their tasks in the field.

The oxen with great oaken yokes resting on their necks just behind the curving horns are brought to the field, and the iron-tipped plow is attached to the yoke. First, the land must be plowed under to give it a respite from last year's growing. It has done its work and deserves a rest.

The plow buries last year's stubble to enrich the soil, and the freshly turned earth is exposed. The deep furrows that lie between the corn rows begin to appear. They will serve as drainage for the spring rains.

The father, being the strongest, holds and guides the plow so that the furrows will be uniform. The eldest son urges the oxen forward with a goad, a wooden staff with a blunt nail imbedded in its tip. When the son prods the oxen, they move forward with an unhurried gait. When the time comes to turn the plow for its return furrow, the goad is lain flat across the horns.

When the field has been plowed, a harrow takes the place of the plow and proceeds to break the clods of earth into workable soil, so that the field will be level. When the field is level and ready for planting, the oxen are turned to pull the great wooden cart with man-sized wheels. The cart is filled with manure gathered from the winter's sheds and mangers. The father mounts the cart to scatter the fertilizer or leave it in mounds for the women to rake. Because metal rakes are expensive, the women use hand-whittled rakes to spread the lumps of manure.

When the field is declared ready for planting, the women and the younger children plant the corn by hand, seed kernel by seed kernel, with three feet between each kernel and three feet between each row.

Because planting time is also family time, the workers at noon rest and picnic under the spreading branches of an oak that grows on the edge of the field. Only the children betray their weariness. The adults must not mention it, because the planting is far more serious than temporary fatigue.

At dusk, when the work is done and the field is pronounced ready for the growing season, the family trails home. The women have their houses to run and meals to be cooked for all. The children go to sleep early, because the next day is a school day. Only the grandmother is allowed to sit by the fire and rest and think her private thoughts about the day's homage to the land that is the family's life.

In the Basque Country, there is an equality between master and servant that dates back to feudal times. When the rest of Europe was caught up in serfdom, a Basque had to be paid for his work.

Even today, if a patron commands a worker to be at a certain place at a certain time, the Basque will show up but work badly. If the patron tells him to show up when he can, the Basque will work his heart out for him.

There was a Basque *paysan* in the new appliance store in the village today. He was dressed coarsely, but still he had an air of some prosperity about him.

There were two models of washing machine in the store, and the merchant was explaining the difference between them to the *paysan*.

"Now, this one is *semi-automatic*," the merchant said, relishing the new words. "You must pump the water in by hand. Then you turn this knob to start the machine that will wash the clothes. And when the clothes are washed, you must pump the water out again by hand."

"I can understand that," the *paysan* said.

"Now, this second machine is *fully automatic*," the merchant said. "Regard this row of knobs. When you turn the first knob to *Fill*, the machine pumps the water in by itself. But you must remember to come back and turn the second knob to *Wash*. The machine will then wash the clothes. Then you must come back again to turn the third knob to *Rinse*, so that the machine can rinse the wash. When you come back to turn the fourth knob to *Empty*, the machine pumps the water out by itself."

The *paysan* asked the merchant to repeat what he had said, but it did not seem to have much effect. "And which one costs the most?" the *paysan* asked.

"The *fully automatic* machine, of course," the merchant said.

The *paysan* regarded him incredulously. "It seems very strange to me," he said, shaking his head, "that the machine which is the most complicated to operate is also the most expensive."

The Basques who live in tiny villages live always in the presence of death. When they go to Mass or Vespers, they must walk through the graves that surround the church. When they are married or there is a funeral, they walk through the churchyard. Often, the churchyards serve as social centers for picnics or as children's playgrounds.

No wonder the villagers regard death philosophically. The graves are always there to remind them of their mortality.

A Basque once sold his soul to the Devil, with three conditions:

Before the Devil could claim his soul at the end of the Basque's life, he must first sit in a Basque chair for a day. Second, he must climb a Basque pepper tree. Third, he must permit the Basque to take his *txirula* flute to Hell. The Devil agreed to all three conditions.

When the Basque died, Satan sat in a Basque chair. But because it was so low and uncomfortable, he could not bear to sit in it for an entire day.

When Satan climbed the Basque pepper tree, he got stuck and had to have help to get down.

Finally, when the Basque took his flute to Hell and played it, all the furnace stokers put aside their shovels so that they could dance.

Disgusted, Satan kicked the Basque out of Hell, thereby breaking the bargain. No Basques have gone to Hell since.

I love the slow sound and tempo of old, creaking carts with great wooden wheels, pulled by oxen.

The carts are hand-hewn out of oak, with a big singletree with a hook that clasps over the yoke, which is also hand-hewn. The yoke sits on the neck of the oxen against their horns, the bases of which have been bound by leather to protect them from the rubbing.

I have worked with my cousins in the fields, haying and planting corn and potatoes. The oxen pull the plow that cuts furrows in straight lines, following the contour of the land.

In season, they are hitched to the massive cart that will carry the hay and crops to the protection of a voluminous barn. Clouds are leaden, and the air is so heavy and dense that it threatens to rip violently apart. And finally, it does. The sky opens silently, and the rain comes down like a cloudburst. But by this time, the cart and its contents are inside and safe.

My cousins have explained to me that the oxen are started in training when they are about four years old. The first time they are in yoke, they accept it as if it were their lot in life. When they are turned loose from the cart for a rest, they are still yoked together. Their heads with wide, curving horns swing in unison even when they feed, as if they were born to that, too. It is like a symphony of movement.

When the *paysan* walking beside the cart lays his wooden goad flat over the base of the horns, the oxen stop in their tracks. When the *paysan* lifts the goad, the oxen resume their forward movement.

Watching them, one would think it was the *paysan* who is setting the pace. But actually it is the oxen who do, plodding ever forward unhurriedly.

It is as though the pace of life on a small Basque farm is geared to that of its oxen.

"Is that our destination?" I asked, pointing at a mountain peak hazy with distance.

"No," the shepherd said. "That is barely the beginning. Is it too far for you?"

"I'll make it," I said in answer to the shepherd's challenge. "And so will my wife."

The shepherd nodded in approval, but the challenge remained. "We will see," he said.

We were in the high mountain province of Soule, where my father had been a shepherd boy. The Basque men are taller here and the country steeper than what we had encountered in Basse-Navarre. It was the day set for driving the flocks of sheep to their summer pasture in the Pyrenees. Unlike in Basse-Navarre, where we had followed one flock from valley floor to the grassland where the timberline ends, here several flocks would go together. They were distinguished from each other by colored powder daubed on their backs—red, blue, green, and black.

The flocks had congregated at the hamlet of Saint-Engrâce, perched on a steep hillside. This was the starting point for the annual trek to the high mountains that bordered on Spain. The sheep were graceful animals with aristocratic faces and long wool that hung nearly to the ground. When summer had advanced and the sheep had become accustomed to the cold nights, they would be sheared by the shepherds who tended them.

The shepherds' necessities of spices and sugar and coffee and wine and sundries were packed on mules that were tied head to tail for safety's sake, much like mountain climbers bound to each other in their scaling. The shepherds in black berets, woolen coats and trousers, and sturdy mountain shortboots had one thing in common. Each had a long black umbrella hooked to the back of his coat collar against the frequent summer showers.

The path to the high peaks grew steeper the longer we climbed. We went through dripping forests covered with green moss and lichen. The worst was yet to come. There was a narrow rising plateau that led to the divide. On one side, the gorges dropped off fantastically into a chasm more than a thousand feet down.

Vultures made their nests in the rock walls, banking downward in great sweeps. I could not help wondering wryly if they fed off the bodies of sheep and shepherds and untried visitors who slipped off the goat path we were following. Mercifully, we climbed into a mist that obscured the awful depths.

The shepherds seemed not at all bothered as they tee-
tered on the brink of the precipice while they were light-
ing cigarettes and visiting with each other. Occasionally,
the lead shepherd who had had his doubts in the village
far below glanced back to see if we were all right. I was
not all right, but I vowed that I would die trying to finish the passage. My wife, who is slender and athletic in
her own fashion, seemed to be having less trouble than I.

The ground leveled off when we came into a little al-
pine valley with the snow patches in startling contrast to
the tender new grass of summer. There was a lone
shepherd's hut in the valley, made of myriad small stones
wedged together. One of the flocks and its shepherd
broke off from the caravan here. This would be his solitary domain for the summer months.

We crossed the valley and entered into another pass
that again skirted a sheer precipice. Something frightened
one flock of sheep and their little rush sent rocks clat-
tering down into the interminable depths. By this
time, my leg muscles were fluttering like leaves and
threatening to give way, and I was sorely tempted to
sit down on the trail and remain there until the home-
ward passage caught up with me. The doubtful shepherd saved my pride by pointing to the green prairie
ahead of us. Tiny streams coursed through the prairie-

like veins, and a cluster of shepherds' huts signaled our destination.

While the several flocks of sheep scattered to their familiar feeding grounds on the great prairie, we stopped at one central hut where the shepherds together would gather for a midafternoon lunch. Ours had been prepared for us by one of my cousins in the village. But first, the doubtful shepherd wanted to offer a toast of Pernod liqueur to the end of the long climb. And to the fact that we had managed to make the trek without turning back.

I learned that this was the land and this was the hut where my father had lived and tended sheep when he was a boy.

And I learned something else. The doubtful shepherd revealed that he and I were related. He was my cousin. He had waited to see if I could finish the passage before he would claim our blood tie.

There is an old Basque adage that goes, *Eskualdun-Fededun,* which means, *A Basque is loyal.*

I had wondered about the origin of the saying until I heard the story about a stern Basque priest who died and went to Heaven. Saint Peter met him at the gate and said, "What have you got to say about the way you treat your parishioners?"

The priest, unrepentant, said to Saint Peter, "Who are you to talk about betrayal? You denied Jesus three times."

I was to learn that Saint Peter has not yet been forgiven by the Basques. To say the least, he is not held in high regard.

I had learned early on that the Basques are unwilling to talk about their beginnings, unless their roots are illustrious. If poverty has been part of the past, the door to inquiry was shut to me. Yet what I wanted to learn was how America had treated their forebears who had gone there to work, and if they had found the opportunity denied them in the Basque Country.

Paul Narbaitz was refreshing in that he spoke the unvarnished truth. I had asked him if his father had found life difficult in his ten years herding sheep in the American West. He said with perfect frankness, "No. Here in the Basque Country was where it was difficult." He proceeded to tell me why.

His father's family had been very poor *paysans* trying to eke out a living on land that did not even belong to them. Paul's father was hired out as a *domestique,* a servant, when he was barely out of boyhood. He worked as a shepherd's helper in the mountains above the village. He lived on corn, from which he made bread, and skim milk left over from making the cheeses that supported the shepherd. He was not permitted even to drink whole milk from the sheep he tended and milked. He was denied the meat his young body needed, and he was lucky if he tasted wine once a year, and coffee ever.

For clothing, he dressed in rags, and one thin woolen cape was his protection in storms and his bed when he slept on the earthen floor of the shepherd's hut. He went barefoot or wore wooden shoes when he had to walk over rocky ground.

It was the 1920s, and the era when Basque men and boys went to the United States to herd sheep. Paul Narbaitz's father went as an indentured servant bound to repay his passage from the wages paid him by a Basque sheepman. He accepted that as a matter of course. What was more important was that the sheepman bought him sturdy shoes, Levi's jeans, a thick woolen coat for winter storms, and an American Stetson hat. So equipped, he felt as rich as a prince. Hard work, blizzards, blazing desert heat, and solitude did not bother him in the least. He had known far worse when he was a growing boy in the Basque Country.

"My father worked ten years as a sheepherder in the American West, and he saved every penny of his wages," Paul Narbaitz said. "The money he made started our family, and we are still benefiting from it."

While he was talking to me, he was leaning on a fence post that was strong as a pillar. Behind him, I could see green pastures where fat cattle and sheep and pigs grazed together, and a newly whitewashed house of stone and tile. His children were playing in an immaculate front yard as if they had no worries in the world.

Paul Narbaitz's father's legacy was very much alive. He had been the true founding father of a respected family that had lived the American dream and brought it home with him to the Basque Country.

When first we came to Saint-Jean-Pied-de-Port, I wondered at the presence of a grand gray stone chateau with turrets and towers and gardens. It loomed over the village like a reigning house.

Since the Basques do not recognize aristocracy within their society, I asked how the chateau had come to be. Did it represent nobility? Finally, I learned that the reason for its existence was not nobility, but ingenuity.

The chateau was built by a great-great-grandfather who had served as a marshal in Napoléon's *Grande Armée*.

When Napoléon's troops invaded Spain, the marshal harangued his troops with the admonition: "We are going to war, but we will make war like gentlemen. There will be no raping, no pillaging, and above all, no looting."

The order sufficed for the French soldiers, but there were also Basque soldiers under his command. The marshal added one further order in the Basque language, which the French could not understand: "Take everything you can get your hands on, and remember that one quarter of what you take goes to me."

The Basque troops of course obeyed him, and the marshal came off best of all, with the wherewithal to build his grand chateau.

I learned one other thing. The Napoleonic Wars are long over with, but Basque villages have a long memory.

Among the Basques, to ask for a written contract
implies a lack of trust. A man's word is a thousand
times stronger because it commits his honor.
The written law is intended to bring order to society,
but the Basques already possess that
with unwritten tradition.
—Old Maxim

DUTY

The Basques don't have much use for those
who don't do their duty or fulfill their obligation
to family. These ne're-do-wells are relegated
to inscrutable silence and oblivion.
        —Old Maxim

The house on the mountain was unchanged from nearly two centuries ago. It rested in a perfect saddle between two hills that rose sharply in back to the high peaks. Deep forests of beech and oak and growths of heather surrounded it on all sides. There were no roads to it from the valley floor below, only steep, winding trails over hedgerows and through the stands of trees and thick berry bushes.

This was one of the ancestral homes of my father's family in the high province of Soule, and because of its remoteness from things modern, it was as poor as poor can be. Yet it was a house that the family was proud of, so much so that they had invited us American cousins to pass the day and be hosted at a family dinner.

Inside the old stone fence, the yard was thickly covered with fern to hold down the mud of spring. The house was made of stone, too, and roofed with a layer of stone and oak chips mixed together. The stoop was lined with wooden shoes that were not for decoration but for hard daily use by all the family. The shoes were stuffed with fern that served as warmth and protection for bare feet.

The house was divided into two parts joined near

the middle. One part was for the family and the other part was for the animals—two young cows, a pig, and two sheep. The warmth from their bodies helped to heat the family living quarters, in the old Basque way. There was a low beam over the front door, so that I had to bow low to enter into the gloom.

The room that met me was a huge room for cooking and living, and there was a little dining room at the end for special occasions, such as the family dinner where we would be hosted. The big room contained a massive open-sided fireplace with cooking utensils— gleaming brass and copper—hung from chains that disappeared upward into the black maw of the chimney. A flatiron used to keep things warm rested near the coals of the fire. In the spring coolness of the high mountains, the warmth from the fireplace was welcome.

My father's aged sister sat in a chair near the fireplace. She was little and shrunken down but with a deep chest from which a deep voice sounded. Naturally, she looked like my father, with the strong jawline common to his family. Her gray hair was pulled severely back into a bun at the base of her neck. Her forehead was deeply lined, and her face was seamed with tiny lines. Gray eyes like my father's looked out from under deep eyebrows. Her hands were twisted with work, but beautiful in a long-boned way. She was no invalid. I learned with astonishment that one night a week, she would carry the family's wash down to the creek below the farmstead, and after it was wrung out, she would carry it back up to the house in a basket.

There was a building attached to the back of the house. It contained the work implements for the little farm—scythes, axes, a plow, and pitchforks for gathering hay. A wooden cart with high wooden wheels rested near the doorway. And beyond that, there was a pasture where oxen and sheep with great noses and long horns grazed on luxuriant grass. They were the source of the family's income, and twice each month, my cousin Josef and his teenaged son would drive a select few to the village market.

But what I remember most was the dining-room table. It was covered with a handmade Basque tablecloth, lined with chairs newly varnished, and filled with delicacies and bottles of wine for *apéritifs* and dinner. There were homemade paté and butter on bread slices with serving knives stuck into them. When we sat down, it was to a veritable feast of vegetable soup, boiled chicken swimming in tomato sauce, potatoes, and the specialty of the house—milk-fed lamb that had never tasted grass. For dessert, there was Basque cake, cognac, and coffee. What the family could not raise on the little farm had been brought up on Josef's and his son's backs from the village far below.

It was a repast that surpassed anything I had been served in fine restaurants.

Poor-as-poor-can-be, but also as proud-as-proud-can-be.

The time has come to say goodbye to:

—The sounds of morning, of cocks crowing in a
nearby farmyard, of church bells tolling in the village below, of a multitude of birds filling the air with song;
sweet perfume from forever blooming trees, air as soft
and sensual as a child's caress, white morning mists ob-
scuring the mountains until the sun lifts the veil to reveal
green mountains. . . .

—Rainy mornings in winter when wreaths of blue
smoke rise from a hundred chimneys into the clouds
above, the patter of rain on a dun-colored landscape. . . .

—Summer days when the pressure of the coming
storm begins to mount so that your heart is pounding in
your ears, and then the sky cracks with the sound of artil-
lery fire and the rains come down in torrents that hurt
like arrows piercing your skin. . . .

—Girls on the country lanes at night, singing in
high soprano voices, a shepherd boy playing his flute
on some mountain above, a *paysan* walking home to
his farm alone, singing because he is happy with the
world. . . .

—Village men singing melancholy songs in baritone voices over a bottle of red wine in a bistro, black berets planted on their heads and elbows planted firmly on a table. . . .

—Churches with balconies of warm brown wood rubbed soft with the oil of ten thousand hands, men singing from the balconies in deep voices and soprano voices of women rising up from the nave below. . . .

—Valleys with whitewashed farmhouses and red-tiled roofs, and in contrast the stone fortresses of homes and hawk-faced men with sturdy bodies in the high mountains where my father was born . . . .

—The thundering fury of Atlantic tempests on the Bay of Biscay, and the men who brave them, with scarred eyes from flying hooks and muscular arms developed from hauling in nets filled with fish. . . .

—Midsummer Night's Eve, and the fire of Saint Jean, a huge bonfire burning at a crossroads and young men proving their manhood by leaping through the flames, as their warrior ancestors did in primitive times. . . .

—Village feast days when townsmen and country-men sit down together at long wooden tables in the shade of oak trees, drinking from bottles of red wine in tumblers. . . .

—The kitchen in the house where my mother was born, and the chair at the corner of the fireplace where she loved to sit, watching the fire that burned behind the gray polished steel of andirons, shining brass candlesticks on the mantle, rafters overhead with glorious hams cured with red pepper hanging from them, and the manger next to the door, neat and clean, holding a gray cow and a pig with shoats suckling noisily away. . . .

—Distant farmhouses of whitewashed stone bordered on one side by vineyards and on the other by tiny figures of grazing sheep. . . .

—Schoolchildren going home at the end of the day with arms locked, dropping off one by one at the country lanes until there is one boy left who walks alone and sings to the sunset. . . .

—Funeral corteges through the heart of the village, the priest in his white surplice leading the procession, acolytes with candles walking behind, men in black suits carrying the casket, which is covered in macabre fashion with a black pall decorated by a skull and crossbones, women bringing up the rear of the procession, praying in audible voices that make a monotone. . . .

—Deep forests of oak and beech and chestnut, cas-

cades of water flashing down to form green pools
where the shadows of trout move like phantoms. . . .

—Vineyards and gnarled vines straightened with
stakes in orderly lines, resembling an army of
wounded soldiers walking on crutches. . . .

—Walking alone along a country lane at night under the uncertain light of a gauzy moon, past barns
pungent with the country smell of cattle and sheep
and pigs and a wind whining through the bare
branches, and coming upon a draft of warm wind that
is familiar out of some forgotten memory of a hundred
years ago, telling you that you have walked this country lane in a life gone by.

AN ALBUM OF PHOTOS

FROM THE

Basque Country

Robert Laxalt and his father's aunt,
Gabrielle, in Arretalepho.

Robert Laxalt's cousin Margarite, in Saint-Étienne-de-Baigorry, Basse-Navarre.

Fishing fleet in Saint-Jean-de-Luz, Labourd.

Street scene in Saint-Jean-Pied-de-Port, Basse-Navarre.

Farmhouses in Basse-Navarre.

Village priest playing handball with the boys in *Saint-Étienne-de-Baigorry*, Basse-Navarre.

Picnic in the churchyard grave in Basse-Navarre.

Countryside scene outside Tardets, Soule.

Monday Market Day in Saint-Jean-Pied-de-Port, Basse-Navarre.

Monday Market Day in
Saint-Jean-Pied-de-Port,
Basse-Navarre.

Hillside barn in *Soule*.

Palombière, Lecumberry, Basse-Navarre.

Author's family tomb in Saint-Étienne-de-Baigorry, Basse-Navarre.

Outdoor Mass for the blessing of the sheep and sheepdogs, Basse-Navarre.

Pilgrim arriving at the chapel of Saint-Sauveur above Saint-Jean-Pied-de-Port, Basse-Navarre.

Chapel of *Saint-Sauveur* above Saint-Jean-Pied-de-Port, Basse-Navarre.

Lunch after the *Shepherds'* Mass.

Men arriving for the Shepherds' Mass at the chapel of Saint-Sauveur above
Saint-Jean-Pied-de-Port, Basse-Navarre.

Knights Templar ruins near Roncevaux.

Fête Dieu in Iholdy, Basse-Navarre.

Robert Laxalt (far left) helping his cousin in gathering cut hay in Ascarat, Basse-Navarre.

Loading the hay into the barn in Ascarat.

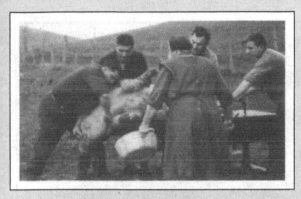

Pig slaughter outside
Saint-Jean-Pied-de-Port,
Basse-Navarre.

Sheep shearing in Saint-Jean-Pied-de-Port, Basse-Navarre.

Sheep leaving the village for summer high pasture in Saint-Jean-Pied-de-Port, Basse-Navarre.

Shepherds moving sheep to the
high pastures in Soule.

Shepherd's *kayola* in Soule.